OVERPROMISE
AND
OVERDELIVER

RICK BARRERA

◆ ◆ ◆

OVERPROMISE
AND
OVERDELIVER

◆ ◆ ◆

The Secrets of Unshakable
Customer Loyalty

PORTFOLIO

PORTFOLIO

Published by the Penguin Group
Penguin Group (USA) Inc., 375 Hudson Street,
New York, New York 10014, U.S.A.
Penguin Group (Canada), 10 Alcorn Avenue,
Toronto, Ontario, Canada M4V 3B2
(a division of Pearson Penguin Canada Inc.)
Penguin Books Ltd, 80 Strand, London WC2R ORL, England
Penguin Ireland, 25 St. Stephen's Green, Dublin 2, Ireland
(a division of Penguin Books Ltd)
Penguin Books Australia Ltd, 250 Camberwell Road, Camberwell,
Victoria 3124, Australia
(a division of Pearson Australia Group Pty Ltd)
Penguin Books India Pvt Ltd, 11 Community Centre, Panchsheel Park,
New Delhi – 110 017, India
Penguin Group (NZ), Cnr Airborne and Rosedale Roads, Albany,
Auckland, New Zealand (a division of Pearson New Zealand Ltd)
Penguin Books (South Africa) (Pty) Ltd, 24 Sturdee Avenue,
Rosebank, Johannesburg 2196, South Africa

Penguin Books Ltd, Registered Offices: 80 Strand, London WC2R ORL, England

First published in 2005 by Portfolio, a member of Penguin Group (USA) Inc.

1   3   5   7   9   10   8   6   4   2

Publisher's Note: This publication is designed to provide accurate and authoritative information in regard to the subject matter covered. It is sold with the understanding that the publisher is not engaged in rendering legal, accounting or other professional services. If you require legal advice or other expert assistance, you should seek the services of a competent professional.

LIBRARY OF CONGRESS CATALOGING IN PUBLICATION DATA
Barrera, Rick.
Overpromise and overdeliver : the secrets of unshakable
customer loyalty / Rick Barrera.
p. cm.
Includes index.
ISBN 1-59184-061-9
1. Product management. 2. Brand loyalty. I. Title.
HF5415.15.B37   2004
658.8'343—dc22   2004053489

This book is printed on acid-free paper. ∞

Printed in the United States of America
Set in New Caledonia

To my father, Enrique,
who had the principles of TouchPoint Branding
in his bones and taught them to me
in our family restaurant.

To my sons, Hunter and Dylan,
my perfect angel genius children, who have been
infinitely patient and understanding during
the process of writing this book.

Acknowledgments

A very special acknowledgment goes to Joel Ehrenpreis, my president of strategic partnership, without whom this book would not have been possible.

This book also would not have been possible without my wife, Keely, who has been a believer and a supporter since its inception.

Thanks also to my mentors and friends, Tony Alessandra, Clay Christianson, Dr. Frank Colleca, Stan Davis, Jim Gilmore, Dr. Peter Kaminski, Ed Keller, John Lee, Stan Leopard, David Morrison, Joe Pine, Adrian Slywotski, and Phil Wexler, who have taught me to see the world in new ways.

A special thanks to Bob Kantor for the heads-up on the Blue Man Group; Deanne Ryder, who helped with the initial research and training design; Barbara Saunders, who did exhaustive research to ensure we had the right agent and publisher; and, of course, my agent, Helen Rees and the superb team at Wordworks, Inc.

Thanks, too, to Brad Davis, Craig Davis, Bill Ehrlich, Kerry Killinger, Terry Onustack, Deana Oppenheimer, Sheri Pollock, and Genevieve Smith at WaMu, and to Denny Clements, Jill Dittrick, John Klein, Jason Schultz, Mike Wells, and Perry Wong at Lexus.

I also want to thank Karen Belgard, Frank Bianco, Patti Bianco, Jack Blumenthal, Bob Braddick, Judy Case, Holli Catchpole, Bob Cestaro, Ron Cox, Jim DePolo, Joe DiPasquale, Paul Duffy, Jean English, Korky Kantowski, Bob Lowry, David Perkins, and Dave Zerfoss for their assistance, support, and friendship.

I would also like to acknowledge my clients, who have allowed me to work and learn in their companies.

Contents

PART ONE

OVERPROMISE

◆

*Meet TouchPoint Branding, the approach that
turns also-rans into winners, and it all starts with a
compelling brand promise. This section shows you how
to craft your own unique promise based on a thorough
understanding of your market.*

CHAPTER 1

What's Going on Here?

Everyone Can Overpromise and Overdeliver!

HARD TIMES CREATE amazing successes. Despite all the talk today of an oversupply of goods and services, industry consolidation, menacing imports, stalled prices, and shrinking margins, a few remarkable businesses have discovered how to make their brands irresistible to more and more customers. What is the secret of their success? More to the point, how can you apply what they have discovered to your business to make your products and services irresistible to customers?

After studying these thriving businesses, these contrarians, I've identified their key strength: a new approach to branding that beats the competition because it's infinitely faster and less expensive than any of the traditional methods. As this book will demonstrate, it is also far more accessible.

For the majority of the examples that follow, I've selected major brands and larger companies because they are more accessible when trying to build a shared understanding of the concepts. The principles of overpromising and overdelivering can be applied in exactly the same way with smaller companies, and in wholesale, retail, business-to-business, and business-to-consumer contexts. You can also overpromise and overdeliver within a company. Divisions, departments, project teams, sales teams, customer service teams, and even individuals can and should define a radically different brand promise and then overdeliver through their products, systems, and people. If unshakable loyalty is your goal, overpromising and overdelivering should be your methodology.

For reasons that will soon become clear, I call this approach TouchPoint Branding. As you read the following cases, see if you can figure out what they have in common. (You'll have the answers before the chapter is finished.)

◆ How do you sell ten million dolls with a conspicuous lack of national advertising?

That's the breathtaking breakthrough of American Girl, a business that started as a tiny direct-mail operation in Middleton, Wisconsin, in 1986, and now sells more dolls than anyone except Barbie. American Girl's first retail store, near Chicago's Magnificent Mile, grosses far more than either of its mighty neighbors, Ralph Lauren and CompUSA. Some fifty million people receive company catalogs, millions more visit the Web site, and, altogether, American Girl sales for 2003 came to $344 million. For girls between the ages of seven and twelve and their families, this company has become a unique source of entertainment and education, a brand that has achieved nationwide recognition and approval.

American Girl doesn't simply sell handsome, eighteen-inch-high dolls. It offers the "whole world," as the corporation's literature puts it, of each of its eight fictional characters: their clothing, furniture; all sorts of accessories; a series of books for each doll that tell her life story and adventures; and a selection of preteen clothes that match those worn by the characters. The Margaret "Kit" Kittredge doll, for example, is a nine-year-old growing up in Cincinnati, Ohio, during the Great Depression. The Kit books describe the hardships she and her friends encounter, the plucky way they solve their problems, and how "Americans opened their hearts" to help one another survive the terrible economic slump. Other dolls include Kaya, an eighteenth-century Native American, and Samantha, from the Victorian era. Signing up your child for the entire Samantha package—doll, books, furniture, and clothing—will set you back $995, and that doesn't count the upkeep. If your daughter wants her doll to have a new hairstyle, for instance, the price at the Chicago store, and at its new sister store in New York City, is twenty dollars.

It's an expensive proposition, yet American Girl has sold more than ten million dolls and more than one hundred million books since its founding. And it has done so without peddling the dolls at other stores and with a bare minimum of paid advertising, largely local-store ads. How, you may well ask, is that possible?

Pleasant Rowland, the founder, tapped into a long ignored but obviously rich vein among preteen girls and their mothers by firmly grounding the enterprise on the premise of wholesome, girlish innocence. Rowland, a former educator, was convinced that girls these days grow up too fast, and that an antidote was needed to the girlhood role model represented by the likes of Britney Spears. She wanted her Pleasant Company and its line of dolls to teach history and inspire girls to learn strength and resourcefulness from the dolls' stories, which Rowland calls "the heart of American Girl." (Rowland sold her company to Mattel in 1998.)

The books are researched carefully and well written. The story of the doll Addy, for instance, was written by respected novelist Connie Porter. Set in 1864, it tells the tale of an African American girl who experiences both slavery and emancipation. In general, historians praise the research and authenticity of the American Girl books but lament their simplifications of history and muted treatments of conflict and violence. Another complaint comes from feminists, who bristle at the dolls' stereotypical roles and emphasis on beauty. But from the beginning the line struck a chord with its intended audience, and the marketing, almost entirely by catalog and word of mouth, has been astonishingly successful. Less than twenty years after its founding, the organization claims that 95 percent of all American girls between seven and twelve know about its dolls and books.

The home store in Chicago has become a shrine for the seven million girls and their mothers who have visited it from around the world, and the New York store, opened in time for Christmas 2003, might well surpass it eventually. Both stores are huge, lavishly appointed, and beckoning "girl places," appealing strongly to girls of all ages and descriptions. They feature smartly decorated restaurants offering classic teas and luncheons, comfortable restrooms, sleek marble floors, and lush red velvet couches that invite mothers and daughters to read a book or simply share a quiet moment.

In addition to the historical dolls the stores offer a line of contemporary dolls in twenty-one combinations of skin, hair, and eye color, as well as the popular Bitty Baby and Angelina Ballerina dolls and accessories. Each historical doll inhabits her own miniature world flanked by glass showcases that display authentic period artifacts to make the doll's world seem real. Each doll also comes with countless accessories. The "girl of today," for example, has (among her many things) a computer that works, a karaoke machine, a martial-arts outfit with various colored belts, a picnic spread, hiking equipment, and skis—not to mention a cast in case she "breaks" her leg while skiing. There's also a full line of clothing that allows girls to dress like their dolls. And the displays are backed up by stacks of complimentary, brightly colored, postcard-sized pictures of each item that are suitable for saving or handing to Grandma when she asks for gift ideas.

Girls and their mothers flock to the stores for "A Day at American Girl Place" that begins with cucumber sandwiches, cinnamon buns, and chocolate mousse, followed by a fashion show with preteen models. Then they go downstairs to the 150-seat theater for a musical production featuring both modern characters and figures from the historical dolls' stories. The performers sing and dance and reinforce the American Girl themes of resourceful heroines behaving admirably in compelling situations. A girl and her mother can have these experiences, plus a CD of the songs, a doll T-shirt, and $120 in store credit, but it will set Mom back $250.

Few stop there, however. A recent visitor at the Chicago store, from Wisconsin, her eight-year-old in tow, bought two ninety-dollar dolls, several books about each, and an array of accessories. The bill came to $650, more than twice what she had planned to spend. "It's a racket, but it's a good racket," she cheerfully told a *Forbes* reporter. "The kids get strong historical role models and stories that teach them a lot about life. You actually feel good spending the money."

So of all these tactics, which is the real secret of American Girl's success?

◆ How did Google become a global verb in only three years?

No, it's not spelled like "googol," which means the numeral 1 followed by 100 zeroes, but it might as well be. Launched in September 1998, Google has become a supernova of the Internet. It is one of the five most popular Web sites in the world and executes half of all the world's Web searches. The gateway to more than 4 billion Web pages, it is also home to more than 150,000 advertisers. Google's long-awaited announcement that it would go public came in the spring of 2004, creating the kind of market excitement that had been missing since the tech-stock meltdown four years earlier. And Google has won society's ultimate accolade by having its name turned into a verb: Surely you've Googled someone or been Googled in your time.

Yet it might never have happened. When Sergey Brin and Larry Page, graduate students in their twenties, first developed a better way to run a search, they tried to sell it to Web portals, including Excite and Yahoo! There were no takers. When they received a one-hundred-thousand-dollar check from a would-be investor, it languished in a drawer for weeks. Since Brin and Page hadn't bothered to set up a corporation, they had no bank account to put it in. Once they took care of the formalities, though, they had a company that was well on its way to becoming a winner. Within four years Google had captured 33 percent of all global English-language searches. It has its home page set up in ninety-seven languages, including Klingon, Latin, and Urdu. And while the dot-com industry in general waded through still more red ink in 2003, Google earned over one hundred million dollars in profit on one billion dollars in revenues. In fact, thanks to disclosures the normally tight-lipped founders had to make as part of the planned initial public offering (IPO), we now know that Google has been in the black since 2001, and will probably be valued at around thirty billion dollars when its stock is sold to the public.

The amazing levitation of Google is already the stuff of business legend. It is the story of a service that has captured the allegiance of millions of people worldwide and leveraged their support into a huge source of advertising income. Yet the company is a throwback to the days of dot-com gusto and glory, a Silicon Valley nest of geeks in cluttered, toy-strewn offices with a grand piano in the lobby. They call their campus, in Mountain View, California, the Googleplex.

The heart of Google is its search method, a set of algorithms that can search through those fourteen billion Web pages in 0.2 seconds, on average. (If a person could perform the same task, taking just one minute per page, he or she would need 5,707 years to finish.) Brin and Page got their initial edge by devising a way to rank the quality of a Web page according to the number of links it has to other pages, which thus focused Google searches on the page most likely to be of greatest importance. Other search engines can now match Google's technique and speed, but Google counts on its long lead and established record to stay on top of the market.

It has other assets as well. One is its way of marketing the ads that bring in most of its revenue: Rather than selling random space on its pages, Google asks for bids on specific words and phrases that appear in customer searches, and hitches the winning advertiser's display only to results of those searches. That way the advertiser can choose a phrase related to his or her product and be sure the searcher has an interest in what's being offered. What's more, the advertiser pays Google only when a searcher clicks on the ad.

Google is also careful to keep searchers happy. Its prime assets, its people maintain, are the users' trust and attention; a search shouldn't take long, and users shouldn't be distracted or annoyed by intrusive advertising. So, unlike other search engines, Google never sells its search results to companies that pay for preferred positions. Its home page is starkly understated, with no flashy graphics and seldom more than thirty-seven words of text. Its ads are restrained, without pictures, pop-ups, or gaudy display type, and a maximum of eight clearly labeled ads appear on a page of ten search results. And if an ad doesn't attract a specified minimum of clicks from searchers, it will be bumped, the theory being that showing people things they're not interested in is a good way to kill the business.

Google's ten thousand networked computers can handle more than eight million searches per hour, and capacity is constantly being increased. The company is also remarkably transparent. Anyone who wants to take the trouble can open up Google products still in development and take them for a spin. With Google Smackdown, for instance, you can compare the number of citations in those more than four billion Web pages for any two contrasting words: "War" references outnumber mentions of "peace," and "money" beats "love"—but not by much. Sure, Google researchers say, competitors and random hackers can see what we're doing and steal or even sabotage promising technology. But the advantages of enlisting the whole world in Google's research and development are so overwhelming that they outweigh the risk.

True to geek principles, there is no strategic planning department at Google. Innovation erupts when someone has an idea that's judged promising. And Google isn't marketed. Instead, its staff observe and listen, poring over figures on searches and results, trying to improve links between sites and their judgments about their relative importance and studying the e-mail they receive to find out what users want. Ten full-time employees do nothing but read e-mail, looking for complaints and relaying them to staffers who can fix the problems. User feedback is essential to pinpointing the areas that need attention.

Google still taps only half of the Internet; another three billion pages are tucked away in unlinked computers or behind corporate firewalls. In the long run Page, Brin, and Eric Schmidt, the company's chief executive, dream of having access to the whole Internet, along with billions more pages of archival material, and searching it all so efficiently that every user finds exactly what he or she is looking for—every time. They know that will never happen, if only because people will always run searches for "spiritual enlightenment." But it's a goal worth chasing.

Okay, we know Google started out with an impressive technological insight, and we also know that the breezy Silicon Valley style that doomed all those other dot-coms somehow hasn't hurt it. But what specific techniques have lifted it to such heights so rapidly?

◆ How do you make people want a gizmo when they don't even know what it does?

TiVo knows the answer. TiVo makes the magic box that has changed television viewing forever for 1.3 million American families. That's not many, a scoffer might say; there are 109 million U.S. households. Right. But TiVo's biggest achievement—and the reason it is exploding from a profitless company with revenues of $141 million in 2003 into one with widespread success—is that most of those families have at least one member who knows what TiVo can do and really wants to try it.

TiVo is a company, and it's also the name of a DVR, a digital video recorder. Unlike the videocassette recorder perched atop your television set, a DVR makes it genuinely easy to record an entire TV show for viewing later. Or, if you're watching a television program and the phone rings, it allows you to pause the show and resume viewing later without missing a thing. You can also let TiVo record the first fifteen minutes of a show before you start watching and then fast-forward past the commercials. You can stop the action and rewind for your own instant replay. You can tell it to record every episode of your favorite show, and it will continue storing up episodes all season long. It can record two shows that air at the same time. And after it's been working for you long enough to learn your tastes, TiVo can suggest a few other programs you might like. What's more, TiVo is working on pairing its recorder with a DVD (digital video disc) burner, so that a customer can copy a show from the recorder's hard disk and archive it in a permanent library of stored performances.

Chances are, you already knew most of that, because you have heard about TiVo on *Friends,* or *Live with Regis and Kelly,* or *The Tonight Show with Jay Leno.* You may have seen the episodes of *Sex and the City* in which Miranda, the attorney, vowed to give up men in favor of her TiVo, because it understood her far better than any man ever could.

That was marvelous publicity for TiVo, but the company didn't pay a cent for the product placement. The writers of *Sex and the City* just thought TiVo was a hot product that added a humorous plot twist. The mention by Leno was less serendipitous, but only a bit more expensive: He was one of a group of showbiz and sports celebrities who got TiVo service free of charge in hopes they would bestow influential endorsements. More than one promising gadget has tried the same promotion strategy, to no avail. Why did TiVo succeed? Because it's a terrific product. The people who try it can't wait to tell you how, for the first time ever, it puts them in charge of their television sets.

But TiVo, the company, had to learn the hard way how to get its message across. Founded in 1997 in Alviso, California, it spent $178 million on sales and marketing, including a national television advertising blitz, in its first five years—only to wind up in financial trouble and with a disappointing number of subscribers. The celebrity-endorsement strategy was born of necessity after the stock market crash squelched any further prospect of using Wall Street money to subsidize price cuts or marketing costs aimed at creating a mass market.

At its high end, TiVo is a pricey gadget, costing $399 for hardware that can store up to 140 hours of programming, plus $12.95 a month for the service. But early in 2004, the company achieved its goal of getting the price of its basic forty-hour model down to the magic figure of $199. Meanwhile, as TiVo engineers strive to make the box ever easier to use, Mike Ramsay, the company's chief executive officer, is busy forging partnerships with big players such as AT&T, DirecTV, and Sony, in hopes of incorporating TiVo software into their products, similar to the way Intel got its chips into computers. Sony is already using TiVo in a video recorder it is marketing in Japan, and DirecTV and AT&T are offering set-top boxes that enable users to have TiVo service also.

TiVo is also trying to encourage word of mouth by organizing parties, Tupperware style, to which current customers invite their friends to watch such major events as the Super Bowl and Oscar night. The goal is "to build a new category and brand and change human behavior on a mass scale . . . on a shoestring budget," Brodie Keast, a TiVo senior vice president, told *Fast Company*'s Scott Kirsner. The parties let nonusers sample TiVo's capabilities first-hand in a comfortable setting with trusted friends—but without the hard sales pitch associated with Tupperware parties. Although copycat products pose a problem for TiVo, its strategy appears to be working: TiVo signed up its millionth subscriber late in 2003, beating its own time line, and then expanded its customer rolls by a whopping 33 percent in the first three months of 2004.

Sure TiVo has a nifty product, but so do lots of companies that no one can name. What is it, exactly, that has brought TiVo to the brink of the kind of success many entrepreneurs can only dream of?

So What's the Connection?

When I first started studying these brands at the request of a client I was perplexed and curious about how such a diverse group of companies had managed to build their brands so quickly and inex-pensively. What could explain their remarkable success? Was there actually an approach that these breakaway businesses shared? If so, was it something that could be helpful to all sorts of enterprises, whether old or new, large or small? I set out to find the answers.

What I discovered was that American Girl, Google, and TiVo weren't isolated cases. Dozens of similarly surprising brands—names like Altec Lansing, Best Buy, Blue Man Group, Cardiac Science, Chico's, Diesel, HardiPlank, Hummer, Samsung, and Washington Mutual—now virtually own their respective markets. As noted at the beginning of this chapter, these brands—which thrive in all sorts of sectors, from manufacturing to wholesale to retail—have been built far more quickly and inexpensively than brands that rely on tradi-tional approaches, most notably advertising. How? They overpromise *and* overdeliver.

Promises Made

Part of what makes a company like American Girl or others you'll read about in the following pages so successful is its ability to craft unique, attention-grabbing promises that radically differentiate it from its competitors. (Think of it as "outpromising" one's competitors.) American Girl promises dolls that enchant girls and teach them how to live a life of substance. Google vows to lead you to virtually anything you want to know—in 0.2 seconds. TiVo's pledge is: TV—your way! And in a crowded business environment in which everyone seems to be shouting the same message simultaneously and at peak volume, exciting, breakthrough brand promises like these are the best way to stand out from the throng.

New companies must develop unique brand promises to battle their way into the marketplace. Established businesses, faced with fighting off upstarts and differentiating themselves from their rivals, have to periodically overhaul their brand promises to adjust to changes in their environments, their competitors, and their customers.

After brand promises have been established clearly, managers need to get their entire organizations aligned to deliver flawlessly on those big promises and, above all, consistently, every day, with every sale or interaction.

Why? Because a promise is, by definition, a serious commitment, a pledge to do or deliver something by a particular time, without fail. Now, I've just told you that you want to overpromise, which may strike you as a little crazy. After all, any business can promise the moon or anything else, from instant sexual potency to thin thighs in thirty days.

But not just any business can deliver when it overpromises, and that's where you have the advantage, because you are going to do things differently. When you overpromise you are putting your whole reputation for honesty on the line. You are saying that you are confident your brand will perform, and you've made a solemn contract with hundreds or thousands or millions of customers. If even a few customers find you reneging their contempt may well spread like a California wildfire. A wise manager knows that trust is the hard currency of business success. The price for squandering trust—sabotaging a brand's promise—is always too high to pay, because at the end of the day, the priceless intangible called integrity is the richest asset on any company's balance sheet.

In the simplest terms, then, capturing customers is all about creating brand promises and keeping them. But in today's tougher-than-ever markets both the promises and the means you use to keep them must be truly outstanding: imaginative, dynamic, unique. Just as you can't merely promise but must overpromise, simply keeping your promise isn't enough. You must overdeliver. You must give your customers more than they ever expected from you. This book will draw on case after case of unusually rapid success to show you how to create and keep your own breakthrough brand promise, the kind that can separate your product or service from the look-alikes struggling in the shadows of anonymity. And just as important, if not more so, it will explain how masterful use of three distinct contact points—I call them Product TouchPoints, System TouchPoints, and Human TouchPoints—can help you overdeliver your promise to customers and inspire their unshakable loyalty.

The TouchPoints

In researching breakthrough businesses I found that what separates business winners from the also-rans is that their key customer contacts came at three different types of moments of interaction between a customer and a brand, or TouchPoints.

Product TouchPoints occur where customers interact with the product or service a company is selling. In other words, these

TouchPoints describe contacts in which the customer actually experiences, handles, buys, uses, and disposes of a product or service, and they are the primary factors in most buying decisions. For Google, a Product TouchPoint occurs every time a visitor types in a query and gets a search result. When a little girl hugs her American Girl doll, reads its story, changes its clothes, or shows it off to her friends, Product TouchPoints are manifest. For TiVo, Product TouchPoints occur when a viewer uses its features—controlling his or her television experience by recording and playing back shows, pausing or replaying scenes, and skipping commercials.

It almost goes without saying that Product TouchPoints become less powerful as products and services become commoditized. When one airline's flight hardly differs from another's, or when two brands of laundry soap are virtually the same, the user's experience plays only a small part in the decision about which to buy. But I assume that you are intent on avoiding commoditization by differentiating your product, so Product TouchPoints will be essential for you. Taking your cue from breakthrough brands such as Google, you will make sure your customer's experience is fresh, clean, and unadulterated by false economies in the secret mix, or uncluttered by intrusive advertising in the search results. Or following the lead of American Girl, you will work to keep expanding the number of wholesome experiences your customer can have with your product or service. And like TiVo you will try to stretch your customer's experience into new product areas and strive to come up with innovative pairings of products and services. In other words, you will offer a really big promise, and then deliver it in a really big way.

Human TouchPoints occur when the customer directly interacts with an organization's people. As you will soon come to understand, I believe that most companies rely far too heavily on human interactions. But I am not in favor of eliminating them. They make it possible to deliver on your brand promise in ways that only fellow humans are capable of—for instance, by empathizing with customers, clearing up misunderstandings, and tailoring solutions to a customer's particular circumstances. It is at the Human TouchPoint that frontline people can bend, and sometimes break, the rules in a customer-friendly fashion. The sales and service people at American Girl stores represent the Human TouchPoints at their respective locations.

When it comes to Human TouchPoints Google is different from the other companies I examined. In fact, it is close to my exemplar of a business that relies very sparingly on Human TouchPoints. Other than through its highly limited, interactive help lines Google customers have no access to the enterprise's people.

At the other end of the spectrum are organizations such as the Ritz-Carlton hotel chain, based in Chevy Chase, Maryland, that have built their brands on their overpromising, overdelivering frontline employees. The brand promise at the Ritz, whose fifty-seven hotels and resorts span the globe, is not clean sheets and an edible breakfast, but rather its incredible standards of human service with a smile. No staff member is allowed to say or even think "That's not my job," and the lowliest busboy is authorized to spend as much as two thousand dollars to solve a guest's problem. The hotel manager will pick up the phone if it rings three times unanswered. To support its Human TouchPoint the hotel chain spends about 10 percent of its payroll on training and education, four times the hotel industry average.

And does this extreme attention to service pay off? Because the Ritz-Carlton is a subsidiary of Marriott International, a breakdown of revenue and earnings figures is not available. However, we do know that the Ritz-Carlton is a two-time recipient of the Malcolm Baldrige National Quality Award and has been recognized for its sterling service by numerous hospitality industry and consumer organizations, including *Business Travel News* and J. D. Power & Associates.

System TouchPoints include all other points of contact between a company and its customers. They occur when customers encounter processes (paper invoices, for example, and frequent-buyer programs) or systems (technological tools such as ATMs and Web sites) that facilitate transactions and interactions. A System TouchPoint is in play when the American Girl catalog arrives at a customer's doorstep, or when a customer shops for a doll on the company's Web site, or still another when a little girl visits the restaurant or picks up a postcard-sized picture of a doll's new costume to show to her grandmother.

Seattle-based Amazon.com, which racked up $5.26 billion of revenue in 2003 and had operating income of $270.7 million, is a prime example of a business whose online retailing systems and processes are so intuitive and so helpful that its customers seldom have any need for traditional customer service. They find what they need and order it, get progress reports by e-mail, pay online with their credit or debit cards, and get their goods by express shipment. It is here, by the way, in the promise of technology, that companies can make their biggest gains in overdelivering, by reducing the variables that hinder consistently excellent service.

All three TouchPoints are vital to an organization's success, though to differing degrees. All three require a substantial and continuing investment of funds and managerial energy if they are to do their job properly, although I should point out that you don't have to be a billion-dollar corporation or have access to vast sums of venture capital to build a terrific brand. Small and medium-sized organizations can do it as easily as large ones—and sometimes even better.

Leighton Dorey, a real estate broker in my hometown of San Diego, has differentiated himself by using TouchPoint Branding, and it has paid off. In 2003, Dorey and his associates sold their properties at 98 percent of list price in only 31 days, compared to a zip-code average of 91 percent of list price in 129 days. Key Touch-Points are: a slick brochure mailed to twenty-two thousand potential buyers; accurate floor plans done by an architect, aerial photography, inspections, and reports before the home is listed; and an interior designer who "stages" sellers' homes.

What counts is not the size of the organization, but willpower—the determination to take your company's brand to the heights by honing the TouchPoints needed to fulfill the brand promise. I can't overemphasize how important the job is. There is no point in laboring to devise a unique brand promise if you aren't going to go the extra mile to overdeliver.

Why, exactly, is TouchPoint Branding so superior? Because it erases that age-old barrier to companywide excellence: insularity. In too many companies, when a brand promise is created, it's created at the top of the organization, but fulfillment is left to frontline employees, who either don't quite get the promise or lack the products, systems, skills, and tools to carry it out. When promise and delivery are disconnected brand value is derailed before it ever leaves the roundhouse. But when the whole organization is pulling together to fulfill the brand promise, brand value becomes a reality. My research shows that properly executed TouchPoint Branding enables managers at every level to inspire their employees to overdeliver on the company's brand promise. This is the breakthrough that can revitalize your company, just as it has propelled the trailblazers you will meet in this book.

What's Next

The promise of TouchPoint Branding is both clear and powerful: It can enable you to build your brand far more efficiently and economically than you ever could with traditional advertising-based marketing. How, exactly, do you go about it? It's all in your over-the-top brand promise and TouchPoints—and you create them based on a thorough understanding of your market.

In the chapters just ahead we embark on a detailed tour of TouchPoint strategy, starting with the basic building blocks—brand and brand promise—and how you can tailor them to your best advantage. So turn the page and let's get started.

CHAPTER 2

What's a Brand Promise?

WHENEVER I SPEAK to a business audience, the first question is invariably: "How do I start TouchPoint Branding?" And my answer is always the same: "From start to finish and everywhere in between, the key to TouchPoint Branding is a breakthrough brand promise." Sure you have to do everything you can to support and reinforce that promise by developing a superb set of Product, System, and Human TouchPoints, but the differentiating promise itself is where it all begins and ends. In fact, despite the thousands of words I've devoted in these pages to crafting and fine-tuning your TouchPoints, you can't even begin to think about them until you have the promise in place. The promise is the axis around which all else revolves. Once you've determined your brand promise, you can see how your TouchPoints align (or not).

It's no overstatement to say that a great brand promise makes all the difference between success and failure. When a brand stands for something truly valuable it vastly multiplies a product's value. In essence, a great brand promises something so unique and useful—so much of an overpromise—that customers reach for their wallets.

What happens to a product—even a wonderful product—when it tries to compete without a brand? In a word: oblivion. Almost without exception unbranded products soon become commodities doomed to compete on price alone because they fail to stand out from competitors or exemplify any special value in the customer's mind.

But this fate is hardly inevitable. Every so often a stalled innovation—a good product without a brand—is rescued by some dramatic intervention. Typically, it happens when determined marketers go back to square one and identify what they should have recognized in the first place: the product's real selling point, not the one they pursued to near disaster.

This is the story of HardiPlank, now a celebrity brand in the home-building trade but once a floundering product. How its makers finally focused on their real customer is a classic tale of necessity begetting invention. How they developed the right promise and then delivered on it at each critical selling stage is a triumph of TouchPoint Branding.

The HardiPlank story began in the 1980s when James Hardie, an Australian building materials company, figured out how to use fiber cement for house siding. It was a huge coup: Fiber cement is less brittle than ordinary concrete and almost indestructible. Sheathed in HardiPlank fiber-cement siding, a house is impervious to fire, rain, snow, hail, salt air, and insects, including termites and carpenter ants. HardiPlank is guaranteed for fifty years against warping, buckling, swelling, splitting, delaminating, and rotting. It comes in various widths, shapes, and surface textures, including cedar, and unlike vinyl siding HardiPlank can be painted and repainted.

A surefire product? Hardie certainly thought so. In 1989, with great fanfare, the company eagerly launched HardiPlank in the North American market.

Result: zero. Builders just wouldn't buy fiber-cement siding.

They preferred vinyl siding because it was easy to install and was touted as outlasting wood. In reality, HardiPlank was much tougher than vinyl. But no matter. It was unfamiliar to builders and therefore resistible. As they told it, HardiPlank was a bust—too heavy to work with, hell on power saws, immune to hiding framing errors.

Ironically, competitors saw the virtues of fiber-cement siding and quickly produced their own versions. But given the product's reputation, even builders venturesome enough to use the stuff demanded deep discounts. For nine dismal years price cutting seemed to be Hardie's only way to compete in North America.

The end seemed depressingly near in 1998 when Lewis Gries, president of James Hardie USA, took HardiPlank back to the drawing board. Here's what he and his team did.

PROBLEM: How do you rebrand a superb product that end users won't buy?

HYPOTHESIS: Something is wrong with our original premise.

PROCEDURE: Conduct rigorous research to check out all aspects of the original premise.

FINDING: Consumers love wood but don't want maintenance hassles. HardiPlank looks like wood but is maintenance-free. HardiPlank is in the right market category and has unbeatable product features.

ANOMALY: The few customers who buy it hate it. Why?

ANSWER: We went after the wrong customers. We focused on selling to builders and ignored end users, our real customers, who have different buying criteria than builders.

As it turned out, the flaw in Hardie's marketing premise was the notion that siding is siding, a matter so boring to most homeowners that they have no strong feelings about it one way or another. This assumption led Hardie to focus its marketing efforts on builders rather than homeowners. Bad move.

Fortunately, Gries and his researchers quickly discovered that homeowners actually do care about siding. In fact, they care a great deal about which materials can best provide the safety, warmth, and security they want in their homes. They also hate the cost and hassle of maintaining other siding materials.

Armed with this knowledge Gries and his team were able to create a brand promise radically different from anything the competition was offering, one that set HardiPlank apart from the crowd no matter how loudly other makers trumpeted their wares. The new approach stressed HardiPlank's psychological benefits, the reassurance that in a stormy world homeowners could curl up safely behind superdurable, weather-resistant siding guaranteed to last fifty years. In short, Hardie promised that HardiPlank is the toughest siding you can buy. It is impervious to everything. It will keep your family snug and secure. And once you install it you'll never have to think about it again. Hence, the brand promise that vaults HardiPlank to the top of the siding market: "It won't rot, warp, or swell. Other than that, it is just like wood. And it is guaranteed for fifty years."

Shrewdly, Gries drove that brand promise into the minds of Hardie's real customers with a three-pronged strategy: public relations (amplified by word of mouth), plus strategic product placement, backed up later by advertising. Aggressive PR got media attention: A national magazine could tell the company's story with far more credibility at far less cost than a company ad could ever achieve. When the ads did appear they served to reinforce the media message. Smart move.

With its new focus and new promise, the company soon won endorsements from leading consumer magazines and trade publications alike—free publicity from impeccable sources, every marketer's dream. *Builder* magazine named HardiPlank one of the twenty most innovative products introduced in the previous two decades, and proclaimed it the best exterior siding anybody had produced over the prior six years ending in 2003. *Midwest Living, Southern Living, Coastal Living,* and *Sunset* magazines, and HGTV, all listed it as the "siding of choice." *Golf Course Living* hailed HardiPlank as the number-one way to add value to a home.

To reach end users directly and make HardiPlank even more visible the company persuaded developers to place its siding on model homes and display it at builder-design centers. Next, Hardie's salespeople reinforced the brand's message by talking it up at large home-building companies, where decision makers had already twigged HardiPlank's favorable press notices. Finally, the company ran ads in *Sunset* and other shelter magazines to sell homeowners on the irrefutable benefits of fiber-cement siding.

Hardie's end run around the builders was predictably effective. After all, if home buyers want something, home builders supply it. That's their business. Accordingly, the demand for HardiPlank soared, leaving builders scrambling for fiber-cement siding at the risk of losing lucrative contracts to competitors. And guess what? All their griping about HardiPlank's alleged defects simply vanished, like a snowfall in April.

Today, HardiPlank is the top-selling siding in the United States. It already protects more than three million homes in North America. Since 1998, sales have leaped by an average 30 percent annually; production has nearly doubled every year since 2000. By making a strong, believable brand promise to homeowners, the company's real customers, Hardie has reincarnated HardiPlank as the third most recognized brand among all building materials.

An inspiring story? A legendary comeback? You bet. But hardly commonplace. In fact, the underside of Hardie's triumph is that it's rare. Most businesses are so blind to brand positioning that they have no idea what they're missing.

The Power of Promise

When I address business audiences I often ask people to share their companies' brand promises. To my amazement, many companies do not have articulated brand promises at all. Those that do often give promises so fuzzy they seem indistinguishable not just from those of direct competitors but also from promises made by thousands of enterprises in any and all markets. These self-deluders tell me their brand promise is "world-class quality" or "guaranteed best service" or "a company you can trust." My unspoken response is harsh: So what? In a world where winners shout distinctive promises these misguided companies whisper sweet nothings and set themselves up to lose.

A generic promise has no meaning to the customer. You have to be specific: First, discover who your consumers really are. Second, tell them exactly how your unique product or service (or both) will consistently meet their needs and unfailingly arrive on time, in order, as advertised. Third, do exactly what you promise—always. Finally, forget about trying to use incremental product or service improvements to win customers to your brand. In a time when every market is saturated and margins are paper thin, small-bore fixes will never be enough to jump-start flagging sales and profits. Success demands that you create a brand promise so radically different from those of your rivals that you first set yourself apart from the competition—and then fulfill that promise.

How?

Brilliantly.

You owe yourself nothing less.

Many businesses are doomed from the get-go. They simply never invest enough time or money to pinpoint their markets, fully identify each significant element of their brand, and craft a unique brand promise consistent with those elements. Neither do they make sure that customers have an optimal experience at each Product, System, and Human TouchPoint; nor do they see to it that the brand promise is fully understood by the organization that will have to deliver on it.

Back to Basics

How to accomplish all that? As with just about every successful venture in life, you have to start with a firm grounding in the basics. In this case that means truly understanding the meaning of "brand."

When I ask audiences, "What is a brand?" I typically hear that a brand is a mark or logo that you stamp on everything you make. It's true that the term branding comes from the practice of searing livestock with the mark of a ranch to signify ownership. But in today's business environment branding has come to mean much more than a way to prevent rustlers from riding off with your property.

The great adman David Ogilvy defined brand as "the intangible sum of a product's attributes: its name, packaging and price, its history, its reputation and the way it's advertised." A brand may also denote the product's relatively straightforward acquisition, financing, ease of use, aftersales support, warranty, and lasting value.

Brands also carry emotional impact; they can connect with a customer's identity and deep aspirations. They can express a buyer's personality, telegraph his or her role in the community and desired social status, and fulfill deep-seated emotional needs. In the end, your brand sets you apart from your competition by the values and attributes your customers believe your product or service possesses and conveys, including its origins and associations.

As you can see, your brand isn't anything tangible. It's not the logo on your product, nor your corporate slogan, nor even your idea of what you do for your clients. Your brand exists only in the minds of your customers. It's shorthand for a host of qualities, features, benefits, beliefs, and business practices that the customer associates with your company, and that he or she is willing to lay out the money to acquire.

Take the Sony brand, for instance. When I ask people what Sony means to them, I get responses such as "high quality," "innovative," "expensive but worth the money," "latest features," "user-friendly," "intuitive interface designs," and "cool electronics." Yet when customers shop for a new DVD player they don't go into Circuit City and say, "I'm looking for a high-quality, innovative, expensive-but-worth-the-money, cool, user-friendly DVD player with the latest features and an intuitive interface design." Instead, they use their shorthand; they say: "I want a Sony DVD player."

So it follows that the only way you can know what your brand is is to ask your customers. Whatever they tell you is what your brand really is. What you think it is doesn't matter (and what you would like it to be is what I call your aspirational brand). The only brand you can own and leverage is the one that exists in the minds of your customers. Perceptions will vary from one customer to the next, of course, and will change over time. Your job is to minimize the variations and the changes by sharply defining your promise and then holding it as steady as possible—until you decide it needs to be changed.

To be truly valuable to customers in today's market, where almost all offerings are high quality, a brand must promise (and deliver) something that is both radically different and better than its competitors. If it doesn't do that you run the risk, as I noted earlier, of consigning your product or service to the burgeoning ranks of those that have been commoditized and are thus being judged on price alone. Slight differences are meaningless, because customers don't have the time to do the in-depth analysis required to make a more sophisticated decision. And please don't tell me your service is better; all of your competitors are promising great service, too. But the only way a customer can know whose service is actually better is to buy the product and wait to see what happens. So customers might as well buy based on price—and, believe me, they will if you can't convince them otherwise.

What's in It for You?

Building the value of your brand is probably the single most important thing you can do to build the value of your company. Legendary investor Warren Buffett (whose name, by the way, is one of America's most powerful brands) has often said that one of the things he looks for in an investment is the strength of a company's brands.

What is a differentiated brand worth? Let's look at the Orville Redenbacher popcorn brand, which has convinced customers that it is different from ordinary popcorn.

The company began by developing a product that was truly different, a hybrid popcorn with kernels that actually popped 10 percent more kernels than existing brands. Then Redenbacher built its brand around the simple claim, "It pops more," backed up by photos of a brimming bowl. Also, selling the popcorn in a resealable jar gave it another tangible advantage over competitors' easily spilled plastic bags. And later, when microwavable popcorn captured most of the market, the Redenbacher brand was so strong and credible that its promise could be changed to "Orville Redenbacher. It's better popcorn."

What does that "better popcorn" translate into in terms of dollars and cents? Huge premiums, that's what. Store-brand popcorn in a plastic bag sells for five cents an ounce, whereas Orville Redenbacher's in a jar goes for sixteen cents an ounce. That's a 300 percent premium. The same holds true, but even more so, for the microwavable variety: The Redenbacher popcorn bags can sell for as much as 700 percent more than various store brands.

Premium pricing by itself is huge, but combine it with high volume and you have the Holy Grail of a highly successful brand. It's tough to achieve but certainly not impossible. As names like Orville Redenbacher, Lexus, Callaway Golf, and Starbucks have shown, crafting the right brand promise and delivering on it can lead to near-legendary status as a company whose products are so coveted that its sales continue to grow even as the price climbs. In short, radical brand differentiation that resonates with customers means enormous increases in profit.

I've repeatedly stressed the idea that your product must be significantly different from those of your competitors. It's also critical that you differentiate in an area that is relevant to customers. It almost goes without saying that the way in which your product or service differs must matter to the people you are trying to attract. Let's suppose, for example, that you're an auto manufacturer whose engine coatings are wildly superior to those of your competitors. If customers don't see your innovation or care about it, they won't choose your brand because of it.

When all is said and done differentiation and relevance create strong brands, and strong brands have the power to increase sales and earnings. Put another way, differentiation and relevance are the basis for financial formulas that determine brand value.

Defining the Promise

Before brand value can be created, of course, your brand has to have a distinctive promise. A promise, as I noted in Chapter 1, is a serious commitment, a pledge to do or deliver something at a particular time, without fail. And a brand promise, in particular, expresses all the things that set your brand apart from the competition, all the characteristics that make it distinctive. But some people confuse brand promises with vision and mission statements, when in actuality they have little in common.

Vision and mission statements are usually created for the benefit of employees, investors, and other stakeholders, and are intended to define the organization's competitive space, its purpose, and its goals. The key difference between brand promises and vision and mission statements is this: A brand promise is created specifically for customers and is built around a product, whereas vision and mission statements are built around a company. Such statements may make something resembling a brand promise in that they signal to customers how the organization will conduct itself, and that's certainly important. But this benefit is only incidental and is nowhere near as significant as the solemn pledge to deliver the array of qualities, features, benefits, and beliefs that the customer expects when it purchases your product or service.

Furthermore, slogans, taglines, icons, colors, or other graphic elements are not the brand promise either, even though they may play a part in conveying it. Such symbols are merely the shorthand reminders of the customer's concept of the brand and the feelings that linger from positive experiences with the organization and its products.

A true brand promise should describe what the product or service will do for your target audience, how it is different from competing offers, and why a potential customer should buy it. An effective brand promise sums up the essence of the brand. For example, James Hardie's brand promise reassures homeowners that their siding will keep them snug and secure for years, while Orville Redenbacher's brand promise simply guarantees popcorn lovers that they will get more of what they love. Whether simple or profound, the promise must be so radically different from what everyone else in the market is promising that the customer hears you even though you aren't shouting. In other words, great brand promises cut through the chatter because they speak directly to customers about an issue that matters deeply to them.

A brand promise also goes far beyond the utilitarian value of a company's product or service and the general category it occupies. A car is not just a means of transportation, and a Lexus is not just a car: Its brand promise conveys styling, safety, luxury, prestige, and the envy of neighbors. A Harley-Davidson is not only a motorcycle but also a way of life that evokes the freedom of the open road and a somewhat rebellious nature. Coca-Cola is more than a soft drink; it is an American icon—and to drink it is to be part of the American experience (which is also why Coca-Cola suffers when anti-American sentiment flares abroad). McDonald's is about food, speed, and consistency, of course, but also clean restrooms and a place where you can feed your kids inexpensively, get them a new toy, and let them blow off some steam in the Playland while you get a much deserved break to sip some coffee or have a sundae. The

Wal-Mart stores brand offers the lowest prices, *always,* and, in essence, promises its shoppers that they can continually raise their standard of living without any increase in income. Based on statistics compiled by the New England Consulting Group, Wal-Mart has more than fulfilled that promise: The group estimates that in 2001 Wal-Mart and other mass retailers reduced the cost of living for middle-market consumers by one hundred billion dollars.

Brands with Great Promise

Every successful brand promise is unique and must be understood on its own terms. All of them, however, spring from a company's thorough study of the experience its product or service gives the customer coupled with a concentrated effort to express the promise both explicitly and implicitly, while making sure the whole organization understands the promise and can deliver on it. The following six cases illustrate the key points:

◆ Cardiac Science's promise of life

Irvine, California–based Cardiac Science is a small company (revenues for 2003 totaled $62 million) that has gone beyond differentiation with a revolutionary brand promise: If you have a cardiac emergency Cardiac Science offers a heart-saving solution. It sells heart-monitoring devices to hospitals and automated external defibrillators (AEDs) to both medical personnel and laymen that enable even people with no medical training to jolt a stopped heart back to beating long before paramedics can reach the scene. "This is the best life insurance you can own," Raymond W. Cohen, the company's chief executive officer, told the *Orange County Register* in 2003.

Cardiac Science is marketing its two-thousand-dollar life-saver device to airlines, schools, factories, police departments, fire departments, and even to individuals with coronary risk factors for use at home or in cars. In cases of sudden cardiac arrest, medical experts say a victim's chance of survival shrinks with each passing second; after six minutes the patient will almost certainly die. But if a defibrillator is used within three minutes of a heart stoppage, according to one study, 74 percent of the victims live. In essence, Cardiac Science's brand promise is the difference between life and death.

It is expected that annual sales of defibrillators will total more than three hundred thousand units by 2006. Cohen predicts that someday defibrillators will be as common as fire extinguishers.

◆ P&G's strategic web

Procter & Gamble claims many of the world's strongest brands, and its latest strategy is to expand the positive experiences customers have with its brands by licensing some of them to partners with compatible, complementary products. The products chosen so far range from Pantene hair dryers (made by Panasonic) to Olay vitamins (Pharmavite) to Cover Girl hair clips and barrettes (Goody Products). These carefully constructed matches involve products picked to mesh smoothly with the attributes of the P&G brands. Hair dryers, for instance, are a natural extension of the company's Pantene hair-care line; Olay stands for beauty, and vitamins extend that promise to good health and inner beauty; Cover Girl's cosmetics adorn faces, and well-groomed hair completes the image.

"We select only products that enhance the brand," Alan Lafley, chairman and chief executive of Cincinnati-based P&G, told *USA Today* in 2003. In 2002, sales of licensed products using P&G trademarks or technology totaled an impressive two billion dollars (overall, the company had revenue of forty-three billion dollars in the year ended June 2003).

The products pay royalties, but the real benefit for P&G comes in extending the brand's promise and reach, creating a web into which the brands can expand. When P&G bought the Iams brand in 1999, for example, it was a pet food line. Now the brand includes licensed pet insurance and travel meals for pets, and Iams is testing licensing of magnetic resonance imaging (MRI) for pets. So Iams is now "a pet nutrition and health company," according to Lafley, one that promises more complete and loving care. And every time a customer uses Mr. Clean household cleaning gloves or Bounty-To-Go paper towels for travelers, the brand's promise is extended and reinforced—even though P&G doesn't actually make the associated products.

◆ Best Buy's better promise

The brand promise of Best Buy Company, a national electronics retailer based in Richfield, Minnesota, is brilliantly conveyed in its name. But the promise was hard to keep in a market crowded with competitors, all of them offering many of the same products at nearly identical prices. Best Buy, which chalked up sales of $24.5 billion in the fiscal year ended February 2004, was headed for oblivion until it scrutinized what it was offering and what its customers needed, which led the retailer to broaden its promise to include a key clause that its competitors were ignoring.

Any "best buy" in electronics, the company realized, had to include computer service and repairs, which retailers, including Best Buy itself, had blithely ignored. In the real world, service is the curse of any personal-computer user, who is left to fume at being directed to voice mail on separate unhelpful "help lines" for each major component of the machine or its software. Customer satisfaction is not the be-all and end-all of computer retailing. The category tops the list of what Sean Skelly, a Best Buy vice president, called "disappoints" in an interview with *DSN Retailing Today*.

Like its competitors, Best Buy had been shipping off personal computers in need of repair to regional repair centers, which meant long waits for already unhappy customers. Now the company offers its computer customers a much more satisfying buying experience, including the reassurance that if anything goes wrong, Best Buy will be there to take care of it.

To deliver on its amended brand promise the company's service experts, known collectively as the Geek Squad, perform nearly half of all repairs in Best Buy stores. They also make house calls for a higher fee, traveling in brightly painted Volkswagen Beetles throughout Best Buy's markets in Chicago, Los Angeles, San Francisco, and the Twin Cities of Minneapolis and St. Paul.

Best Buy has broken the mold with its extended brand promise. It is probably just a matter of time before its competitors are forced to match it.

◆ The cool mockery of Diesel

Selling clothing to young people is only incidentally about the clothes. Attitude and identity are what count most: sexiness for Calvin Klein; earnest social commitment for Benetton; hipness for the French Connection. And for more than two decades Diesel SpA has prospered by poking fun at them all. The Italian company's founder, Renzo Rosso, mocks the whole idea that a certain brand of laundry detergent, soda, clothing, or any other consumer product can make a person's life significantly better. The appeal is to a cool, edgy generation of customers who know perfectly well how marketing works and who want to prove their savvy to anyone hip enough to get the message.

From its headquarters in the Veneto region of Italy, Diesel will parody anyone, from Levi's cowboys to Benetton's social conscience. Models in one ad pout and preen like Calvin Klein's, all the while chanting ironically: "Thanks, Diesel, for making us so very beautiful."

In effect, Diesel's brand promise is a paradox: If customers consume Diesel's wares they will prove themselves superior to the consumer culture. But paradoxical or not, it works. Diesel now sells in more than eighty countries and 120 own-brand stores, with an extended line of licensed goods and even its own hotel, the Pelican, in Miami Beach.

◆ Walt Disney's magical feeling

Not long ago a customer at Disneyland—the Magic Kingdom—asked a street cleaner sweeping Main Street where he could get a cup of ice cream. The sweeper pointed him to a nearby refreshment stand. When the customer got there the counterman said, "I believe you're looking for a cup of ice cream," and handed him one. The sweeper had taken the trouble to radio the counterman—and the delighted customer had another dose of the magical feeling Disneyland aims to give its visitors.

From the beginning Walt Disney designed his theme park to promise a three-dimensional experience of the magical world he had created, as powerful in real life as his movies were in theaters. The park's employees are called "cast members," because they play roles in the performance the guests experience. They are carefully trained and empowered to deliver on the brand promise of a relaxed, family-friendly playtime in a familiar, immaculate, and totally nonthreatening environment.

No detail is too small to matter. The Burbank, California–based Walt Disney company boasts that a discarded chewing-gum wrapper typically litters Main Street for only a matter of seconds before a cast member scoops it up. And the scooper-upper is just as likely to be a vice president as a street sweeper. At Disney, which listed trailing twelve-month revenues of twenty-nine billion dollars as of March 31, 2004, everyone "owns" the brand promise.

◆ Altec Lansing's repositioning

In 2001, Altec Lansing, known as the IBM of speaker systems, had both the strengths and the problems that a comparison to Big Blue suggests. It was making speakers for nearly 30 percent of all personal computers, and its brand and technology were solidly respected. But its margins were under pressure, it faced hot new competition, and a new generation of consumers seldom thought of Altec Lansing when they wanted to hook up speakers to their MP3 jukeboxes.

So the company set out to revitalize its brand promise—and, not so incidentally, to develop a new line of products to fulfill its new promise. With a tripled marketing budget and the help of consultants, Altec Lansing came to a key conclusion: Although most companies in the audio industry base their promises on the technical side—known in the trade as "speeds and feeds"—sound is what matters to the consumer. So great sound became Altec Lansing's new brand promise, with a tagline to match: "Just listen to this!"

In a down market the privately held Milford, Pennsylvania–based company's sales were estimated at $175 million in 2003.

Promises Made, Promises Broken

At this point, a strong word of caution is appropriate: Whatever else you do, make sure you live up to your brand's promise. Nothing kills a brand faster than an empty promise. Just ask Firestone, a unit of Japan's Bridgestone Corporation, which had thousands of tires recalled in 2000 after tread separation was implicated in scores of auto-crash deaths. Besides the immediate costs of litigation and the millions of dollars paid out in victim compensation, the Firestone brand suffered incalculable damage when it lost the trust of consumers who had relied on Firestone tires to perform safely and give them many miles of problem-free driving. Efforts to repair the company's image continued in 2003, when Bridgestone/ Firestone announced that it had settled a nationwide class-action lawsuit by agreeing to spend $15,450,000 on a three-year consumer safety education and awareness program.

Since your brand exists in the collective mind of consumers, it is tempting to use advertising, public relations, and "spin" to beef up perception of the brand. You might try, for instance, to "add value" by making the brand seem youthful, leading-edge, or otherwise appealing to your targeted consumers. But such tactics are not always wise, since sooner or later the customer's actual experience will have to live up to the image. A brand that is found to be largely created from spin will soon be dropped.

MasterCard's "priceless" commercials are a good example of a brand promise that is undifferentiated and basically based on hype. Any credit card can do what the commercial says MasterCard does: enable you to buy stuff. Rather than being a priceless benefit, the ability to buy lots of goods with a credit card is a commodity. Customers know it, and they are voting with their dollars: Visa has gained market share every year since the priceless campaign began.

Smart marketers craft their promise to emphasize the intrinsic value of their product or service offering, reinforcing the promise with the plain truth that the buyer will experience. For instance, Commerce Bancorp, based in Cherry Hill, New Jersey, promises to suit the customer's convenience instead of the bank's—and sure enough, its branches stay open into the evening, seven days a week.

Even a solid, accurate brand promise can come to grief when things go sour. In its early days Intel leaped to the forefront of the microchip business with the tagline "Intel Delivers." The promise was great technology, world-class manufacturing, service second to none, and reliability. And, in fact, Intel delivered—until an unexpected uptick in demand coincided with a stutter in manufacturing.

When Andrew Grove's daily mail started to bring torn-out

copies of Intel ads with the slogan altered to "Intel Never Delivers" or "Intel Delivers If You're Lucky" the chairman called his agency and ordered the promise removed from all Intel ads. Today the tagline is noncommittal: "Intel Inside." Who can fault that? Look inside and, yup, sure is. But the implicit brand promise is that this is the best chip in the business—and Intel still must deliver on that.

It remains to be seen whether Microsoft's brand promise will be severely tarnished by the increasing incidence of devastating viruses and worms that take advantage of Microsoft programming flaws. Customers resent having to download patch after patch to fix problems that should never have made it into the Microsoft products in the first place, and gripes about reliability are standard fare. Microsoft is unique because of the stranglehold it has on computer applications, but continuing problems could very well provide an opening for a competitor to establish a viable competing brand promise.

Fortune Favors the Bold Brand Promise

The only sure thing about creating a new brand promise is that no one can predict its fate. Pioneers are always vulnerable to dangers that those who come later can avoid. By the same token, businesses that are first to develop differentiated promises are in uncharted territory where the pitfalls are unknown. Even a seemingly brilliant new promise can backfire for unforeseen reasons.

Honda once launched a campaign with the slogan "Honda. Follow the leader." Yamaha quickly countered with "Yamaha. Follow no one."

Jeff Slutsky, a speaker and author, often tells the story in his talks of a hair salon whose business was sharply curtailed by someone else's billboards advertising six-dollar haircuts. Then the salon countered with a billboard attack of its own: "We FIX $6 haircuts!" Business soared.

If a new promise is so risky, why bother—especially if your current brand promise is performing adequately? The answer lies in the business history of the last decade: We have seen one marquee organization after another lose its edge and flounder as competitors rapidly stole huge chunks of market share. You must do more than provide quality products or services; virtually every business does that now. The marketplace is so crowded, the competition in every industry so fierce, that resting on your laurels literally risks bankruptcy. There is no safety in playing it safe.

What's Next

You know what you have to do. That great brand promise you crafted so painstakingly only a few short years ago may by now have lost its punch with customers. The competitor who once ate your dust is now running neck and neck. Unless you're willing to be the one pictured in the rearview mirror you need to make some changes. But where do you begin? First, you have to reevaluate your current brand promise. The next chapter will tell you how to do just that.

CHAPTER 3

Understand Your Brand Promise

So often in our lives we're caught short by the seemingly abrupt transformation of someone or something familiar. An awkward, gangly little girl puts on makeup and an off-the-shoulder dress and we suddenly realize that she has metamorphosed into a young woman. A street we've always visited for haircuts, hardware, and groceries has, while we weren't looking, turned into Restaurant Row.

It happens in business, too. Nothing lasts forever, and that includes your brand promise. Changes in the marketplace, in your own shop, and in the tastes and circumstances of your customers make it more than likely that the promise you designed and implemented just a few years ago is no longer in sync with today's reality. The unequaled customer service that once set you apart has now been equaled—your competitors have caught up, and your customers have noticed. Or perhaps the audience you so painstakingly identified as your prime target has aged into a new set of priorities. For whatever reason, things have changed, and your brand promise is no longer as precise and focused as it needs to be if your product or service is to maintain its competitive edge. It's no longer an overpromise.

That's not to say that every change is necessarily negative. Suppose your initial approach called for decent, not excellent, product quality; you never perceived best quality as integral to your brand promise. But since the demise of your top-of-the-line competitor customers have found your product to be more than satisfactory and now regard its quality as an important brand attribute. You have been blessed by serendipity—but you still need to revise your promise to take full advantage of this lucky break.

Where to begin? Like the mechanic who services your car, you have to thoroughly evaluate and understand the complex mechanism of your current brand promise before you can give it the tune-up it needs. That's where this chapter comes in. It will bring order to the task of reexamining your customer offering, particularly the parts that determine your advantages and disadvantages, and help you use your newfound knowledge to update your brand promise in a way that fits your current reality. I would advise you, for example, to assess not just your end product or service, but also the consistency of your operations, processes, systems, core competencies, and know-how, as well as the value of your trade secrets, databases, and proprietary software. Figuring out what effect any changes in these areas have had on the validity of your current brand promise will go a long way toward helping you effectively develop and exploit a revitalized one.

A Few Not-So-Simple Questions

Determining exactly where you stand at this moment clearly requires a rigorous accounting. A successful promise—whether it's brand-new or a rejuvenated version of a previous promise—is not born of a sudden flash of inspiration. If it is to radically differentiate you in a way that is valuable to your customers, it must be built brick by brick, with attention paid not only to the intricacies of products and services and manufacturing and marketing, but to all the constituencies that have to be on board to achieve a breakthrough. That means current customers and potential customers, employees, shareholders, distributors, and suppliers. After all, you will have to live with the promise for a long time. You will have to align all your TouchPoints with it and arrange your entire organization around it. So all the stakeholders whose suggestions and support can make or break your effort must be part of the process.

To start you along the road to a complete understanding of your brand promise, I have devised a number of basic questions for managers that deal with the components mentioned above. And I have included the answers of three companies—Patagonia, Pottery Barn, and Samsung—that have demonstrated a thorough knowledge of who they are, how they got that way, and what their brands offer to customers. Their stories will inspire you to do your own in-depth research and find your own answers. And after you respond to the last question, you'll have a wealth of new insight into your own brand promise. Let's get started.

◆ **What is the essence of your company?**
   Ask yourself why the company was started.
   What was the founder's vision; what did he or she
   plan to do better than anyone else?
   Are you fulfilling that vision now?

Every new business starts with a core idea, a dream, a vision of what the founder hopes to accomplish and how he or she plans to go about it. Perhaps your entrepreneurial dream was born when a personal want or need went unfulfilled for lack of relevant options, or when you noticed that someone else was facing just such a predicament. Or perhaps your vision emerged when you saw how poorly another company was serving a particular market niche; you knew you could do better and swore to avoid your competitor's mistakes.

This first question is a way to get your coordinates, so to speak, to zero in on the real reason you are devoting a major share of your life to making this business proposition work. For, when all is said and done, your passion is what informs your brand promise. An incisive look at what originally started your juices flowing can also tell you whether or not you've wandered off your stated course. Like a wilderness-trail hiker, every so often you need to take a break, look at your map, and check your compass. Otherwise you risk becoming dangerously lost, or ending up someplace you never intended to be and won't like when you get there.

Our first case study, Patagonia, is a terrific example of how a company's essence can inform its brand promise, and how a savvy and successful company makes sure it retains a valid understanding of that promise even as the world around it changes.

Patagonia was founded a half century ago by a young mountain climber, Yvon Chouinard, after he became disgusted with the quality of existing pitons, the metal stakes used to anchor rock-climbing ropes. Chouinard, a blacksmith by trade, hammered out a new kind of piton that was not only far stronger but reusable, which meant that mountains around the world would not be festooned with rusting bits of metal. Chouinard's piton revolutionized climbing and eventually begat Patagonia, which, with its parent Lost Arrow, went on to offer rugged clothing and accessories for outdoor sports lovers, from climbers to skiers to bikers. The company's brand promise: "We provide for environmentally responsible adventure."

In some ways Patagonia's brand promise and its success evolved from a paradox: The founder's intense passion for mountain climbing and his great love of the outdoors led him to campaign for a scaled-down version of the sport—fewer climbs and climbers, simpler tactics, and less equipment—so as to preserve the vertical wilderness. Chouinard preached purity, simplicity, morality, responsibility, and restraint, hardly the watchwords of American business and surely not a textbook case in the art of selling. (Contrast Chouinard's stance with that of the snowmobiling industry in the current battle over closing Yellowstone National Park to their machines. Can anyone imagine a snowmobile company leading the fight to ban snowmobiles in order to protect the park's wildlife and decrease air pollution?)

But what might seem like a wrongheaded approach to retailing proved to be the cornerstone of the company's success. Serious climbers recognized that Chouinard's concerns were well-founded. Mountains were being defaced and the overuse of gadgets and the degeneration of climbing styles were threatening to destroy the adventure of the climb and the appreciation of nature that are vital to the sport itself. Chouinard's insistence on high quality—"defects could threaten a life," notes the company Web site—coupled with his dedication to preserving the environment resonated with his target audience. The company has continued to grow and now sells its products through specialty retailers, a catalog, a Web site, and forty of its own stores. It raked in $220 million in sales in 2002, $17 million more than in 2001.

In the midst of what appeared to be resounding success, Yvon Chouinard decided to take stock. He ordered an assessment of the company's manufacturing operations to gauge their effect on the environment. His conclusion: The company had veered off course, lost sight of its environmental underpinnings. In short, Patagonia's brand promise needed an overhaul. Determined to do his part to protect the environment, Chouinard switched the materials used in the company's clothing, opting for organic cotton, which is grown without the use of pesticides that can pollute groundwater. Sure the clothing would cost more, which might crimp the company's sales, but Chouinard was adamant: "Now that we know [the environmental harm], it would be evil for us to do anything less."

A big part of the reason Chouinard's do-the-right-thing approach has worked so well is his constant effort to know who his customers are, to understand how they think, to make sure the company doesn't lose its relevance in a changing world. To do that he keeps abreast of lifestyles and market trends as he hatches new product ideas. What he knows for sure is that his customers are very much like him and very much in tune with the essence of Patagonia: passionate about the environment and eager to enjoy outdoor adventure, but always mindful of mankind's duty to protect the earth. As the company notes on its Web site, "It is the style of the climb, not the attainment of the summit, which is the measure of personal success."

> ◆ **What are your brand's most important attributes?**
> **What do customers think of when they hear your**
> **company's name? Poll your customers to see**
> **if their answers match yours.**

When you first framed your brand promise, you and your customers may have been in complete agreement about your brand's most important attributes. But internal changes in systems and processes or changes within the operations of your suppliers and distributors can cause a breach. So can modifications in rivals' offerings. Customers' perceptions and expectations about your brand can shift because of positive and/or negative experiences at any one of a number of TouchPoints.

A customer's interaction with your brand doesn't begin, after all, when she picks it off the shelf. Her attitudes have been influenced by word of mouth, by your advertising and public relations, by her feelings toward the store where she bought your product, or perhaps by a conversation with your customer-service personnel. Customers may feel strongly about matters you never even think of as being attributes of your brand. Your company's decision to endure a strike rather than increase hourly wages, for example, or its sponsorship of a television show about breast cancer may lead some customers to express their feelings (positive or negative) with their pocketbooks.

These are the kinds of connections you will need to explore to get a fix on your current brand promise. Pottery Barn, a home-furnishings mecca that is now a division of Williams-Sonoma, executed the process brilliantly a few years back when it decided to launch a Web site.

Begun as a single store in Manhattan in 1949, Pottery Barn now boasts 159 outlets, not counting its 56 Pottery Barn Kids stores. It also operates a direct-mail business that distributes 98 million catalogs a year, and it has launched two profitable new catalogs in recent years: *Pottery Barn Bed + Bath* in 2000 and *PBteen* in 2003. In each case the company created special products for the rooms featured in the new catalogs. The company's overall success reflects its ability to fulfill its brand promise: "We help you create a cozy, stylish home at affordable prices."

Before beginning its Web site in July 2000, Pottery Barn asked its consulting firm, Prophet, to make the kind of basic brand study that I encourage you to do. As Laura Moran, a Prophet director, told *Target Marketing* magazine, "Before we could translate the brand to a new medium, we had to know what the brand was all about." So Moran and her staff began by asking questions of customers and a cross section of employees and managers, including the leaders of design, merchandising, and customer service. She concluded that the brand promise and the company's self-image did indeed mesh: Customers came to Pottery Barn for "a cozy, stylish home at affordable prices."

But Moran also learned that the brand promise included a pledge to share Pottery Barn's expertise with customers whether or not it led to a sale. In its stores and catalogs Pottery Barn gives customers a vision of a lifestyle that is comfortable and classy without being fussy or expensive, and it supports that vision by endeavoring to build a helpful, trusting relationship with its customers.

As a result of her research Moran advised her client to include a variety of "whole-room environments" on the Web site that transcend what customers can see in stores or in the catalog. So that the site would support the brand's pledge to share its expertise she also urged Pottery Barn to add a "design studio" feature with practical information on everything from folding a cloth napkin to cleaning leather furniture.

A few years later Pottery Barn conducted its own major research project among potential customers, laying the groundwork for the *PBteen* catalog. For an entire year the company's designers and marketers interviewed teenagers and visited popular haunts like malls and skateboard parks to investigate their tastes. Patrick Wynhoff, senior vice president of Pottery Barn Kids and *PBteen,* told *Fast Company* that stocking up on teen magazines earned him more than one wary look from puzzled clerks in supermarket checkout lanes.

Important data also came from a Pottery Barn contest in which teens sent in photographs of their rooms. Noting the similarity in the teens' rooms, Wynhoff was struck by their desire to save everything. His revelation led *PBteen* to offer a collection of desks, dressers, and bins that will help these little pack rats organize all their stuff.

The catalog, which is intended for ten- to nineteen-year-olds, is full of beanbag chairs, bed sheets with animal designs, and locker-like desks. Though there are some hip touches, most of the furniture and accessories in *PBteen* are traditional—a bow to the brevity of teen trends and the reality that parents do most of the actual buying. What is more, the catalog's merchandise is true to Pottery Barn's brand promise: It offers a comfortable lifestyle at affordable prices.

My third case study, Samsung, the Korean electronics powerhouse, consciously monitors its brand in a constant, ongoing process so as to fulfill its promise: In electronic design and technology, we deliver the latest and the best.

Samsung has come a long way since it emerged on the international scene with bargain-basement reproductions of other companies' wares. These days its leadership in such technologies as LCD displays and DRAM chips propels it toward the top of the market in sales of big-screen televisions, microwaves, and other consumer electronics. Because Samsung is a vertically integrated manufacturer of hardware that ignores software or content, its products tend to become commoditized. To offset this problem it must offer a constant stream of breakthrough electronic items, which it has successfully done. Samsung's performance has improved steadily, with 2003 sales rising 7.5 percent from the year before to a record $36.9 billion, with net profit totaling more than $5 billion.

Samsung's promise to deliver the latest and the best in design and technology demands constant research into the fickle tastes of its young, hip, gadget-crazy customers. Its products, from TV sets to DVD players to cell phones, have to keep abreast of appearance trends while also breaking new technological ground. To stay in touch with customer tastes Samsung relies heavily on its CNB group, a team dedicated to "creating new business." CNB runs focus groups and conducts interviews to find out how customers and potential customers feel about the company's current products, and what they want in the way of new ones. In these sessions CNB members try to spot changes in attitudes and other signs that may presage a developing trend. Small and sleek cell phones may be the in thing today, for example, but five years from now young customers may covet something larger or more macho-looking. Samsung aims to be ready for whatever its consumers may want.

Given its complete reliance on hardware products, which have a shorter shelf life than software and content, Samsung cannot prosper without a steady flow of appealing new merchandise. To find it, and to make sure the company continues to fulfill its brand promise to provide the best design and technology, Samsung never stops asking its customers what they think and how they feel about its products and the organization itself. It has proven to be a winning formula.

◆ **Ask customers, "Why do you buy our product?" Then ask them, "Why don't you buy our competitors' products?"**

If you think that asking customers why they buy from you will yield the same information as asking them to name your brand's most important attributes, you are wrong. People often buy for reasons unrelated to the attributes they cite.

For example, I have always used one particular brand of toothpaste. I can list several positive attributes, including its decay-fighting formula, its tooth-whitening feature, and its fresh taste, but that doesn't explain why I stick with it. The real reason is that I inherited the brand from my parents, and I've never felt any need to change.

On the other hand, I've also been shopping at the same grocery store for years, but I'm not really satisfied with the place. The lines are slow, for one thing. I could also list some positive traits, such as the pleasant staff, but that wouldn't explain why I still shop there. Simply put, despite my overall dissatisfaction, I'm too busy or lazy to go through the hassle of driving to a store that is farther from my house.

Toothpaste manufacturers may not be able to do much about my brand preference—it's emotional and too ingrained. Customers who buy a product because it reminds them of their childhood are a gift, something to be grateful for. But my grocery-shopping habits are another story; they could change overnight if a competitor built a new store nearby. By the same token, many a mediocre franchise or dealership that held onto customers because it was the only such operation in a particular area has been shocked to discover that customers bailed out to order from the parent company's Internet site. Geography can only carry you so far.

Asking customers why they buy from you can help you identify the kinds of people who are best served by your product or service. Chances are they won't be the ones you had in mind when you created your brand promise.

Let's say you've targeted retired couples as your primary customers. Like some cruise-ship operators, you may have assumed these people wanted to be catered to. But by asking the "why" questions you may discover that many of your current "elderly" customers have little taste for lounging around and being tended to. They want to be out and active. No wonder sales have been dropping. The services you designed to deliver on your brand promise are out of sync with customers' preferences.

Asking customers why they don't buy your competitors' products will bring a whole other set of revelations. To be sure, some of their reservations about your rivals will be routine: The products are too expensive, poorly designed, or often out of stock. But you're also sure to hear explanations that have little or nothing to do with the rival products themselves. For example, a substantial group of your customers may object to your leading competitor's reliance on overseas factories, where pay scales are below subsistence levels. Others might have read an article years earlier that accused your rival of fraud or gender discrimination or false advertising, and they have rejected its product or service ever since. Millions of people around the world have boycotted products of the ExxonMobil corporation, for example, ever since the *Exxon Valdez* ran aground off Alaska in 1989, spilling eleven million gallons of crude oil that killed hundreds of thousands of animals, including birds, otters, seals, and whales. And then, of course, there will be those who don't buy another product because, well, they are simply in the habit of buying yours. Nothing about your brand promise or the way you have fulfilled it has motivated them to look elsewhere, and for that you can be thankful.

But with the new information you've gotten from the "why" questions, you can now set about fine-tuning your brand promise to capture new customers and hold onto the ones you've got.

That's what Patagonia does with regularity. In fact, its brand promise is a work-in-progress. The company is constantly adjusting its products and presentation to address the comments and suggestions it solicits from its very vocal and dedicated customers.

While Patagonia's promise to provide for environmentally responsible adventure has powerful philosophical and emotional content (which I will discuss shortly), it also has a very practical side, one that is grounded in Yvon Chouinard's personal insistence on moral restraint and responsibility. Consider Patagonia's guarantee: "We guarantee everything we make. If you are not satisfied with one of our products at the time you receive it, or if one of our products does not perform to your satisfaction, return it to the store you bought it from or to Patagonia for a repair, replacement, or refund. Damage due to wear and tear will be repaired at a reasonable charge."

The company's design mandate, presented on its Web site, also emphasizes its practicality: "Our definition of quality demands that any garment we make be long-lasting and strong. It should also be as light as possible for its intended uses . . . and be easy to care for. It should be versatile and as unspecialized as possible." The products, like the brand promise, are constantly under review, as the Web site states, based upon "data from extensive lab and field tests as well as the experience of fellow employees and customers."

An example of Patagonia's close connection to its customers' interests and desires can be found at Water Girl USA, one of several separate divisions. As the promotional material illustrates, Patagonia knows exactly who inhabits its target audience. "When you're carving roundhouse cutbacks on your shortboard or throwing ends in your kayak," one piece declares, "you don't have time to fuss with four-four sport tops or shifting bikini bottoms." A few lines later: "We design our clothes to fit and flatter the muscular physiques of athletic women, with sophisticated styles and prints that won't make you look like a teeny bopper."

Many suggestions for product innovations and improvements come from employees, who tend to be outdoor athletes. But Patagonia never stops asking for its customers' views, and it takes them seriously.

◆ **Ask *non*customers why they don't buy your product. Then ask them, "Why do you buy our competitors' products?"**

To reach a reasoned position in politics and government participants need to hear both the pro and con arguments. The same is true in business. That's why you need to interview noncustomers when reexamining your brand promise.

Negative feedback can have positive results—if you are willing and able to put it to good use. Learning that some aspect of your brand promise, or of its supporting products and processes, is driving away a substantial number of potential customers should inspire some serious repair work. As Albert Einstein once observed, "We cannot solve problems with the same kind of thinking that created them. We must first identify failure, and then reverse it."

Sometimes the problems noncustomers cite are all too real, a glitch in the product design, perhaps, or maybe an irresponsible distributor. Correcting these sorts of problems may not be easy, but the sooner you know about them, the sooner you can fix them. Sometimes, though, potential customers stay away because of a misperception about your product, service, or organization, and that's a problem you can repair with an amended brand promise. These noncustomers may have had a bad experience with your product years ago and never realized that the problem had long since been fixed. They may have misinterpreted a word or a picture in an advertisement and sworn off your brand to this day. Your current customers apparently are not bothered by such concerns, at least not enough to complain, so noncustomers are your only source for negative information. Unless you talk to them you'll never know what stands in the way of their becoming your customers.

Noncustomers can also keep you well versed on the strength of your competitors' brand promises, information you need to set yourself apart. Asking noncustomers why they prefer another company's product will evoke a mélange of responses, varying from the practical to the emotional, but they will help you discern the outline of a competitor's brand promise. With that in hand you can then redesign your own unique promise.

That kind of differentiation was not originally part of the Pottery Barn brand promise. When the company first opened in 1949 the furniture business was dominated by big manufacturers like Ethan Allen, and department stores were filled with conservative, affordable, nondescript chairs and sofas.

At first, Pottery Barn operated like many other furniture stores, buying its merchandise from old-line manufacturers and arranging it as a "collection." Eventually, though, perhaps after interviewing noncustomers, the company's leaders realized that middle-income Americans were interested in furniture with more flair and more personality than they could find in the traditional stores. Today more than 95 percent of Pottery Barn's goods are exclusive, created in the company's design center across town from the Williams-Sonoma headquarters in San Francisco. Critics complain that the company's nationwide presence has homogenized home design, but even Pottery Barn's detractors acknowledge that it has made good design more affordable. Which, after all, is exactly in line with its cozy, stylish, and affordable brand promise.

To make sure that it continues to keep that promise Pottery Barn puts great store in its design. Every potential product has to pass a five-point inspection in the design studio: It has to be attractive and modern-looking, but not to the point of making customers uneasy; it must feel good to the touch; it must be of high quality; it has to be durable (that is, childproof). Finally, the designers are asked if they would want it for their own homes or to give as a gift to their best friends; any hesitation and the product is dropped.

Listening to what noncustomers had to say also saved Pottery Barn from what could have been a brand-damaging, public relations disaster in 2001. After a coalition of consumer groups, labor unions, and human rights activists voiced concern about the company's purchase of products from Myanmar (formerly known as Burma), a country whose work practices have been likened to slave labor, Pottery Barn wasted little time in severing its business relationships there. All products made in Myanmar were removed from store shelves, catalogs, and the Web site, and the company prohibited buyers from giving the country any new business. By responding to the criticism Pottery Barn quite likely converted some of its former critics into current customers.

◆ What emotions do customers feel when they buy and use your product?

There may be products that fail to evoke emotional reactions in those who buy them, but I have a hard time thinking of any. Even the humble paper clip can spur me to irritation if it's flimsy, or bring a smile if it comes in a bright color. We react to the objects in our lives, including items on a store shelf or in a catalog, on both an intellectual and an emotional level.

A customer may say she chooses a particular bar of soap because it cleans better, or because the price is right, but she is also reacting to other stimuli. She may have a sentimental association to the soap's scent. Perhaps she believes the soap is popular in the kinds of upscale homes she admires. Maybe she identifies with the heroine of a television show sponsored by the soap company.

The products you use speak volumes about who you are. In our culture we are categorized and judged, at least in part, by the brands we display—the make and model of car we drive, the schools our children attend, the watches we wear. Each purchase is, on some level, an occasion for deciding how we will be viewed by others. Rich and successful? Smart and perceptive? Environmentally conscious?

Advertisers always try to attach a positive image to their products. Some companies use symbols (Mr. Clean); others use humor (talking ducks); and still others use stories (a bank helps a young couple to buy their dream home). When we make our product choices we are reacting to these ads, mostly on an unconscious level.

What emotions does your brand promise trigger? How do your customers react when they see your product? Once again, the chances are good that you don't know as much about their reaction to your brand as you could. Over time brand promises gather associations, negative as well as positive. When a company recalls a product because it is unsafe, or swallows another organization after a long, bitterly contested, and widely publicized battle, the events are incorporated into the brand. Even if you are aware of the troublesome overtones you may not realize, unless you ask, how significant they are to your current—and possibly soon-to-be-former—customers.

Pottery Barn's brand promise is more laden with emotion than that of, say, a paper-clip manufacturer, because it sells products for the home, a place that people care about deeply. Whether it's a tiny apartment in a big city or a rambling house in the suburbs, home is the one place in which we can create a safe, comfortable, welcoming, and aesthetically pleasing space. And most of us will not be satisfied unless that space meets two criteria: It must reflect our own taste and it must meet with the approval of visitors.

By creating a lifestyle brand Pottery Barn has found a way to satisfy both requirements. Its stores offer a mix of home furnishings and accessories ranging from chairs to wineglasses to candleholders, all bearing the mark of the same designers and all fitting into the same sophisticated style and atmosphere. The colors are muted, the style is contemporary (but not experimental), and the quality is high. By any measure, the products are clean-lined and tasteful, and their sum—a lifestyle that has enormous appeal to a wide cross section of customers—is greater than its parts. In a sense, Pottery Barn outfits the American home in the same way

The Gap clothes the casual dresser—in a stylish yet affordable fashion.

Pottery Barn's brand promise acknowledges that furnishing and decorating a home can be stressful by presenting the company as a kind of home-decorating mentor. Salespeople are trained in helping customers to mix and match the furniture and then add the appropriate accessories. The catalog offers plenty of advice, but the Web site's assistance is even more detailed.

At each point of contact Pottery Barn pays attention to its customers' emotional needs. Their anxiety is soothed and their uncertainty resolved, so they leave the store, the catalog, or the Web site satisfied with the experience and pleased with the company that provided it. How does Pottery Barn achieve this virtual retailing nirvana? By paying attention to the emotional elements that play such a significant role in any brand promise.

Samsung is no less concerned with its brand's emotional impact, though it targets a very different customer and seeks a very different reaction. The company's brand promise, offering the very best in design and technology and aimed at young gadgeteers, is intended to elicit a response that can be summed up in a single word: Cool! Samsung wants these customers to be blown away by its cutting-edge products; it wants them to yearn to be the first in their school or on their job to have the latest Samsung.

To deliver on its brand promise the company is entirely focused on achieving technological supremacy. Back in 1999, Texas Instruments presented Japanese companies with new chips that used digital-light processing (DLP). With their million-plus micromirrors flipping at high speed the chips could potentially produce much sharper pictures in projection televisions. But the Japanese companies couldn't find a practical and economically feasible way to produce the TV sets. Late in 2001, Samsung took on the task. Within two years it had seven DLP projection sets on the market at prices of thirty-four hundred dollars and up; they were the top sellers in their price range.

Price is part of Samsung's calculated emotional appeal. Its customers don't expect bargain-basement prices; they understand that you have to pay more if you want the very best. Samsung obliges. In stark contrast to earlier years, the company produces only high-end products, for which its customers proudly pay the price—thus signaling to their friends and families that they are the coolest of the cool.

To maintain and enhance those feelings Samsung has allied itself with that most popular of techie film series, *The Matrix.* Its ads, appearing in theaters showing *The Matrix: Reloaded,* pictured Trinity dropping Agent Smith with a kung fu kick on a screen that rotated to reveal that it was only three inches thick—a forty-inch LCD flat-panel TV from Samsung. Simultaneously, the company was selling a wireless phone that looked just like the one actor Keanu Reeves uses in the film, and which had an even larger presence in the third film in the series, *The Matrix: Revolutions.*

Samsung works hard to make its young customers feel excited and self-satisfied when they buy its products. The company also works hard to stay in touch with these customers to make sure they continue to feel that way. Keeping tabs on the emotional response your product elicits is an important means of keeping your brand promise current.

◆ What effect does your company's reputation have on its brand promise?

Do you worry about what customers think of your company's reputation? You should.

Nike, for example, took much too long to recognize that public criticism of the working conditions of its overseas vendors' employees, which surfaced in 1996, was altering perceptions of its brand. The notion that the corporation didn't care about the inhumane treatment of these workers was firmly planted in many customers' minds. Even though Nike has done much to improve the workers' conditions since then, the impact on sales is still being felt.

Customers can have long memories. More than eighty years ago, Ford Motor Company founder Henry Ford published material that was decried as being anti-Semitic. Ever since, a sizable number of American Jews have boycotted Ford cars. Similarly, companies that continued to invest in South Africa during the struggle over apartheid have lost customers sympathetic to the cause of the country's nonwhite population.

Many companies, on the other hand, have reinforced and strengthened their brand promises by actively pursuing policies that promote positive values and good works. Everything about Patagonia, for instance, its corporate behavior, its interactions with customers, and its products, reflects its ardent commitment to the environment. From the very beginning, when its slogan was "Go easy on the rock," the company and its employees pledged to be responsible residents of the planet.

Virtually all of Patagonia's facilities recycle, compost, grow gardens, have edible landscapes, and minimize the company's use of energy and water. Patagonia encourages carpools, buys only recycled paper, and purchases electricity derived from renewable sources. The same devotion shows up in its manufacturing and distribution, including its reduced use of formaldehyde and its reliance on rail instead of truck transport.

In 1985, Patagonia began allocating 10 percent of its pretax profits to grassroots environmental groups. It upped the ante a dozen years later, pledging to give the greater of 1 percent of its sales or 10 percent of its pretax profits, to ensure that the groups it supports would receive funds whether Patagonia made money or not. Most of the funds have gone to small, community-based organizations often overlooked by corporate donors.

Patagonia's dedication to the environment reflects the long-time concerns of founder Yvon Chouinard, who insists that the company's core values be updated regularly to retain relevancy. "A company that takes the long view, no matter what industry it is in, must accept that it has obligations to minimize [its] impact on the planet," he told the *Puget Sound Business Journal.* "I put together a one-hundred-year plan for Patagonia. And I think there's a good chance the company will last that long. Why? Because we exist for something bigger than the bottom line."

The company's passionate dedication to the environment makes customers feel that by supporting Patagonia they are also supporting its cause. The strong environmental component of its brand promise has been a potent force in separating Patagonia from its rivals.

◆ **If your brand were a person, how would you describe him or her?**
In the same vein, how would you describe each of your competitors?

I'm asking you to anthropomorphize. In ancient times people attributed human characteristics to trees and animals, and we still ascribe human emotions to our pets. Poets and playwrights find that anthropomorphization can free the mind to imagine the world (in your case, your brand promise) from a new perspective, which is why it can be useful to you.

Try this exercise: Compose a letter in which you describe the "person" who is your brand. Is he or she young or old? Large or small? Mild-mannered or aggressive? Straightforward or shifty? Graceful or awkward? Some other avenues to explore: How much schooling does your brand person have? What kind of job? Single or married? How many kids? What kind of house? What kind of car? Favorite food? Favorite sport? Favorite movie? How do they dress? How do they spend their free time and with whom?

When you finish, read over your letter as you think about the market in which you sell and the customer group you are targeting. Would the person you have described be an appropriate salesperson for those customers? Would they buy from this person?

To get you started, here is my image of the Pottery Barn brand as a woman: She is in her middle forties, married, with a daughter in college. She manages a small department in the local department store; her husband sells insurance. Together they earn enough to pay the mortgage on a nicely landscaped, three-bedroom home in a middle-class neighborhood and to keep up payments on their two cars (hers is a Mini Cooper). She is a pleasantly attractive, outgoing sort who is easy to talk to and comfortable with who she is. She loves to dress up and go dancing, but can only persuade her husband to go a few times a year.

Now perform the same exercise for each of your competitors. How do your competitors' brand-people compare with your own? Who is best suited for the marketplace you share?

◆ How do your employees perceive your brand?

Every hour of every day your employees are deciding, consciously or unconsciously, how much extra effort to invest in their jobs. I can think of nothing more important to your company's success than the task of convincing your employees to invest more, rather than less.

Everything your company says and does—from your community relations policies to the quality of your products and services— is part of your brand, and thus part of your employees' brand experience. How they feel about that experience will largely decide how your customers perceive your brand, so you need to know just where your employees stand. Does the existing corporate culture inspire them to do their best? Has your company established standards and incentives tied to employees' support of the brand?

In the last few years, according to the Towers Perrin consulting firm, the boom-time tendency of many employees to focus on stock options and dreams of IPOs has been replaced by a greater concern for the soundness of a company and its treatment of individuals. Many companies, in turn, have begun to recognize the need to mesh the way they deal with employees with the way they present themselves to customers. The object: to earn the trust of employees as well as customers; to develop enduring relationships with both groups; and to deliver better on the brand promise. The immediate benefits include reduced turnover rates, which eventually lower training costs and promote the consistency of employee performance.

In 1999, Pizza Hut, based in Dallas, Texas, put substantial resources into aligning its culture and the treatment of its employees with its brand promise. As a result, the company's turnover has plummeted, and *Communication World* reports that it has been voted the "best place to work in Dallas." The American Express company, too, places major emphasis on employees' connections to the brand, to the degree that every employee's performance review includes an assessment by management of what he or she has done to support the brand.

The Samsung global brand, according to Interbrand, is growing faster than any other. In 2002 its brand value was $8.3 billion, a one-third increase over the previous year. Behind that remarkable record is a corporate culture that inspires every employee to achieve both personal and corporate goals. And an essential part of that culture is a major emphasis on understanding and building the brand. New employees receive elaborate training in the values and qualities of the Samsung brand, and the company monitors how the overall workforce views the brand.

Samsung works in various ways to make employees happy in their jobs and proud to be associated with the organization. Every plant site, for example, has an in-house health-care center to treat employee illnesses and promote physical fitness, with exercise programs tailored to the particular locale. Samsung is an international leader in creating accident-free workplaces, and it boasts company-wide educational and training programs, an integrated disaster-control center, and rescue teams in every location. The company has been hailed as one of the safest workplaces in the world.

Samsung has also become a global leader in creating environmentally friendly products and building pollution-free workplaces. Its reduction in the use of potentially harmful substances in manufacturing and its extensive recycling programs, not to mention its green partnerships with suppliers, have earned the company ISO 14001 certification and a bundle of international awards.

Yet another corporate activity that binds employees to Samsung is its large-scale, international sponsorship of sports events, including the Olympics. On its Web site the company explains this commitment under the heading, "The Ultimate Showcase of Dedication and Inspiration," qualities it clearly wants its brand to be identified with. Sports, the site adds, have "the ability to unify regardless of race, gender, religion or geography . . . at the heart of sports is fair play, which Samsung esteems as a key corporate belief. Through sports sponsorship, Samsung expands its brand recognition and relates an approachable corporate image." In those few words Samsung sums up much of what the company and its employees are all about—and why they have been so successful.

Samsung thinks long and hard about ways to bring employees into sync with its brand promise, closely monitoring their attitudes on the subject. You should do the same.

What's Next

In this chapter I have suggested how you can assess the intricacies of your operation to arrive at an accurate picture of your current brand promise and a clear sense of the attitudes your customers and potential customers have toward your product or service and your promise. Understanding your current situation is the first step toward crafting and keeping a unique and powerful, revitalized brand promise. The theory is, you should know where you are before you make any decisions about where you want to go.

Now you're ready to take the next step. In the following chapter I offer some practical ways to get you to where you should be: firmly positioned to reap the rewards that come with a well-defined, tightly differentiated brand promise.

CHAPTER 4
Make Your Brand Promise Unique

"WHAT'S MISSING?" is a question that's asked over and over again at Husqvarna, a member of Sweden's Electrolux AB group and one of my clients. You see, Husqvarna is on a never-ending quest to fulfill its customers' needs even before the loggers, landscapers, arborists, and other professional users of its high-end outdoor equipment know exactly what those needs are. Headquartered in Charlotte, North Carolina, the North American staff regularly meets with customers on their own turf to learn how Husqvarna can better serve them. And as Husqvarna's own success shows (the company has increased its economic value added by sixfold in recent years), asking questions—and following through with imaginative solutions—is one great way to make your brand promise unique.

A few years back the answer to the "What's missing?" question turned out to be "profits" for landscape contractors. Landscapers typically wage a constant fight just to stay in the black, and Mother Nature is a tough sparring partner. Too little rain and the grass doesn't grow enough to mow; too much rain and landscape crews can't get onto the turf—until the rain stops, that is, at which point they can't mow fast enough to catch up. Early snow or late snow or no snow at all can be a blessing or a curse, depending on whether a landscaper is also in the snow-removal business. Furthermore, the weather and the seasonality of the business heighten the challenge of recruiting, training, and scheduling work crews. And, as if Mother

Nature didn't have enough dirty little tricks in her bag, the high cost of workers' compensation insurance adds yet another burden, as does the constant strain of managing and maintaining the equipment needed to do the job.

Given the high rate of bankruptcy and turnover in the industry, it's no surprise that Husqvarna's servicing dealers were also facing similar profitability issues. Of more than thirty-one thousand outdoor power-equipment dealers a decade ago, less than seventeen thousand are still in business today. The survivors lean heavily on manufacturers to finance their inventories, but shrinking industry margins threatened to put the squeeze on financing terms.

Enter Husqvarna. When the answer to the "What's missing?" question came back "customer profitability," David Zerfoss, the company's North American president, and his team saw an opportunity. By changing their own strategy they thought they could increase profits for the landscapers and dealers. Husqvarna began offering a product line that allows a landscaper to outfit his crews with equipment that shares common parts. The commonality means faster training of workers and technicians, interchangeability of engines and parts for on-the-fly repairs, one-stop shopping for equipment and service, and one-vendor financing with Husqvarna's proprietary credit-card purchase or leasing program.

Not only have cash flow and profitability improved for Husqvarna's landscaping customers, but its dealers are enjoying these rewards as well. Now dealers need only one line of equipment to satisfy their customers, instead of the multiple lines they used to offer. And carrying a single line cuts costs related to maintaining showroom and warehouse space, stocking inventory, and instituting training programs for everything from repairs to sales to handling warranty claims. Another Husqvarna innovation, its Marketing Alliance Program, further reduces dealers' investments in inventory and speeds up inventory turns, boosting profitability still more. As one dealer near Husqvarna's Charlotte headquarters explains, "I was always one bad season away from bankruptcy until I got with Husqvarna. Now I know I'm going to be profitable for the long haul. They've made this a viable business!"

With the inception of its Total Source system, which is unique in the outdoor power-equipment industry, Husqvarna has helped everyone in the value chain earn greater profits while the company better serves both its customers and its partners. And Dave Zerfoss says he's just getting started: "We've been methodically putting the pieces in place for several years. Electrolux, which is the largest manufacturer of appliances and outdoor power equipment in the world, isn't as well known in the United States as it is in Europe, but we are about to change that." Husqvarna's success in the commercial sector has attracted "prosumers," Zerfoss says, which he describes as consumers who want to use what the professionals use. "We are reinventing the industry for the twenty-first century," Zerfoss winds up. "We are on a mission to change everyone's thinking."

Like Husqvarna, you too can come up with innovative ideas by looking at the world from your customers' point of view. But that's not the only way to jump-start your creativity, as this chapter will make clear.

Wiring Your Company for Bright Ideas

Creating a unique brand promise requires a bright idea—a differentiating characteristic that will make your brand unforgettable. This might seem to contradict what I told you in the previous chapter—that "a successful brand promise is not born of a sudden flash of inspiration." That's true as far as it goes. The difference here is that your inspiration, your bright idea, will not really be sudden at all. It will be the product of your deepening understanding of brand promises and the work you are doing to find out what your constituencies really want. In effect, you are laying the fire of a new brand promise, which requires only the spark of your imagination to set it aflame.

Stephen Riggio, chief executive of Barnes & Noble, laid and ignited a new brand promise in 2002 when he decided to offer greater value to the book-buying public by taking the nation's largest bookseller deep into the publishing business. In the process he sparked fear in the hearts of publishers and distributors alike, who worry that the big chain will not only create new pricing pressure at the Product TouchPoint but will also wield undue control over which products make it onto limited shelf space.

In a move designed to differentiate B&N from its competitors while also increasing profits in an industry that operates on notoriously thin margins, Riggio is developing, printing, and marketing his own list of titles—mostly classic fiction, how-to guides, and illustrated books. The beauty of Riggio's brand extension lies in its economic double whammy: Many of his titles are in the public domain and require no royalties or licensing fees to be paid, so he can produce and sell his books much more cheaply and still realize a handsome profit. But if a particular title fails to match expectations, he has much greater leeway to slash prices and quickly clear out unsold inventory—while still making money.

In two years Riggio has traveled almost halfway toward his goal of getting 10 percent of B&N's revenue from publishing its own line of books. And he expects the operation to produce its second year of double-digit sales gains in 2004.

To help you find your own igniter this chapter will suggest general areas to explore in your search for a promising new promise. In other words, it will prepare you to brainstorm for the right bright idea. The ultimate goal is to identify a competitive space with high relevance, a gap that you can fill with a radically differentiated offer, one in which the advantages will be difficult for your competitors to copy in the short run. In a word, an overpromise.

I encourage you to adopt a special attitude toward this task. Set aside the caution you apply when making decisions based on such weighty matters as the unstable economy or your latest profit-and-loss statement. Sure, these are important, but you can relax your defenses, take a more freewheeling approach. The purpose of this exercise is to stretch your mind and let your imagination roam unrestrained. So arm yourself with a positive attitude and get started identifying potential new brand promises.

◆ Probe the gaps in customers' lives to uncover their hearts' desires.

Before you do anything else, find out what your customers' needs are right now and what they expect them to be in the future. But beware the popular approach of simply gathering demographic data on your customers; demographic information goes stale too quickly. Instead, you'll want to delve deeply into the public's collective mind.

Truth be told, most companies don't do the intensive study required for spotting new or developing trends. There are exceptions, of course, like the Target corporation, the Minneapolis, Minnesota–based upscale discounter. Target fields a team whose sole mandate is to figure out what next year's hottest clothing trends will be. Diligence like that pays off. Target's revenues and earnings have marched steadily higher over the last three fiscal years. For the year ended January 31, 2004, total revenue had climbed 9.6 percent from the year before, to reach $48.2 billion, while net income had spurted 11.3 percent, to $1.84 billion.

To craft your breakthrough brand promise you need to figure out what customers are going to want and need in the years ahead. Unlike the questions presented in the last chapter, which aimed at uncovering customer and noncustomer opinions about your current brand promise, the data you gather this time will tell you about people's lives and how they imagine their futures will unfold. Your goal is to hypothesize about long-term trends, because you have to look far enough into the future to give your company adequate time to gather the resources necessary for developing the ideas, processes, and products that will comprise your new and differentiated promise.

Here are some of the questions you should ask current and potential customers: What are the three biggest challenges you face going forward? What's missing from your life right now? How do you think your life will change over the next five years? Ten years? What changes would you like to see? What one product would make your days easier and/or happier?

Answers to these sorts of questions will enhance your understanding of what people want in general, which is invaluable to discovering what they want in particular.

Bernie Marcus and Arthur Blank had an unerring feel for what their target customers wanted and needed when the pair opened the first Home Depot in Atlanta, Georgia, in 1978. Home Depot's original target audience, the do-it-yourselfers, pride themselves on their ability to take care of the jobs that come with owning a home. They balk at hiring others to perform work they can do themselves, not only because outside help costs more, but also because they actually enjoy doing the work. Providing this group with a superstore carrying an enormous range of products (some forty to fifty thousand different items), the likes of which had never before been assembled in one location, was the founders' brilliant and inspired idea. And their understanding of their customers was what enabled them to realize their vision.

How did Home Depot respond when Lowe's and other companies copied its formula and tried to outdo Marcus and Blank at their own game? They expanded on their original bright idea. It didn't take a crystal ball to see that Home Depot's core customers, the baby boomers, were growing older. The new inspiration came when Marcus and Blank decided that the aging boomers might now be amenable to having a little help around the house. So, in addition to free advice, the stores began to offer installations of carpets, doors, and even heating systems at prices below those charged by local contractors. Little wonder that this revamping of Home Depot's brand promise has been a smashing success. From a mere $7 million in sales in 1979, Home Depot could boast $64.8 billion in sales in fiscal 2004 (which ended February 1, 2004), a number that represented an 11.3 percent increase from the year before. Net income, meanwhile, shot up 17.5 percent, to $5.8 billion from $4.9 billion.

In the previous chapter I discussed the major role Pottery Barn's design studio has played in supporting and adjusting the retailer's promise to help customers "create a cozy, stylish home." To be effective the studio's thirty-three designers obviously have to keep tabs on customer tastes and interests. How do they do that? Well, they don't use focus groups like most companies do. Instead, the Pottery Barn designers live their own lives in ways that keep them in touch with the public's changing attitudes. When they dine in restaurants, for example, the designers are urged to observe how tables are set and what styles of furniture are gaining popularity. They make a point of visiting model homes and Realtors' open houses to look for new architectural trends. At flea markets they take note of hot-selling items. The theory behind their on-the-scene research is that customers' design tastes often happen unconsciously. Hence, asking questions isn't sufficient; you have to observe customers' behaviors as they go about the business of daily living.

How you spot the trends that will shape your new brand promise depends upon the circumstances of your particular business. What works for Pottery Barn may not work for you, but the objective is clear enough: Determine what your customers will be wanting at the moment you're ready to unveil a new promise.

◆ **Lead your industry's parade by anticipating new trends.**

Theater professionals distinguish between static characters, the heroes and villains who don't change over the course of a play, and the kinetic ones who are somehow transformed. Hit plays are richly peopled with kinetic characters, because their stories are more true to life and, hence, more interesting to audiences. In a similar vein, kinetic companies rise or fall on their abilities to foresee important trends while aligning themselves and their brand promises accordingly.

When the Internet was in its infancy, for example, a handful of people recognized that the new technology would have a powerful impact on business. They envisioned books, educational courses, airline tickets, even medicines being sold online. They foresaw millions of people playing games, participating in auctions, and developing friendships in faraway places with previously unknown individuals. These seers understood that to one degree or another virtually every industry was about to feel the repercussions of this new, interactive medium. By being out in front of a life-altering trend some of these visionaries made fabulous fortunes.

If you had been reading this book at that time would you have realized how the Internet might alter your industry's trajectory? Would you have understood that such a shift would require you to adjust, if not totally rework, your own brand promise? Would you have had the imagination and courage to perceive and pursue the opportunities?

Eventually, every company that hopes to survive has to reflect what is happening in its industry. So the sooner you anticipate a significant development or a new trend, the sooner your organization can begin to prepare for it and cope with it. But if you want to do more than just cope, if you want to be a leading light, it is crucial that you find out now where your industry is headed over the next ten to twenty years. To put it bluntly: If you're not a bellwether in today's fast-paced, supercompetitive business environment the chances are good that you'll waste your capital on facilities, equipment, and personnel that will be wrong for the long haul. And by the time you discover that your brand promise is hopelessly out of date you will have neither the physical plant nor the appropriate staff to undertake a smooth turnaround. At which point all that will be left is the final blessing, R.I.P.

Industries go through stages. They may first adopt a vertical structure and then a horizontal one, or they may handle all responsibilities in-house for a decade or so before deciding to outsource various processes over the next several years. Whatever the advantages of each organizational method, only the companies that spot a trend early will reap the significant benefits. For instance, a trend-spotter may make its assets "sweat" more, thus shrinking fixed costs and allowing it to slash prices. By the same token, a company that fails to perceive or ignores a trend will be playing catch-up with the leaders for years (if it lasts that long).

The mandate to keep abreast of change, if not lead it, extends to business basics. Are companies from other industries planning to enter your area? Is the supply of raw materials becoming more accessible? Are new vendors altering the traditional cost structure? Such developments can present exciting opportunities as the economics of your operation are recalibrated. Cheaper raw materials or supplier parts, for example, might increase your ability to compete on price—or tilt you toward a more horizontal structure. The key is to notice the clues early and move quickly to seize the advantage that almost always belongs to the pioneer.

The ready-to-wear market for younger consumers used to be divided fairly evenly between The Gap and Abercrombie & Fitch. Then Target arrived with private-label fashions that attracted the coveted Generation Y shopper. Its goods were well made, reasonably priced, and, more to the point, designed to meet that shopper's developing sense of style. Had The Gap and Abercrombie been on their toes, they might have anticipated Target's invasion and prepared better defenses, or adjusted their brand promises to find new targets of their own.

Potential changes in current customers' lifestyles, broader demographic trends, and geopolitical developments can radically alter the realities of competition within your industry. Consider the upheavals that occurred within various industries when two-income families became the norm: restaurant and take-out meals, the need for child care, and second-car purchases all increased.

In the previous chapter I cited Patagonia as a prime example of a company that has flourished by riding the crest of a sociopolitical wave, environmental awareness. The company's founder, Yvon Chouinard, created a company that manifests his commitment to conserving our natural resources. And by recognizing how important environmental concerns are to its sportswear customers, Patagonia was able to seize and retain a valuable business advantage.

◆ Butt heads with conventional wisdom in your search for business opportunity.

Everyone accepts numerous assumptions and adheres to a host of conventions; for example, we obey traffic signals and presume that our elected leaders are competent. But in business, at least, all sorts of customs and assumptions need to be taken apart and examined for opportunity.

Take the assumptions you and your competitors share about how your industry operates, for example. Although everyone may agree on the standards that determine a product's size, composition, or price range, each area represents a potential point of departure, which means an opportunity for you to develop a unique brand promise. Consider coffee shops. Everyone in the business took it for granted that coffee would remain a cheap commodity. Then the

Starbucks corporation came along and turned the common assumption on its head by proving that a trendsetting merchandiser with an original business model could boost coffee prices substantially.

Years before Starbucks broke new ground everyone knew that drugstore soda fountains went unused most of the day except at lunchtime, when they were typically full. Then Ray Kroc, who later put the McDonald's corporation in the annals of business history, suggested to Chicago-based Walgreen's that its soda fountains sell take-out coffee in paper cups during quiet hours (Kroc happened to be providing the paper cups). The take-out idea changed the soda-fountain business along with the daily habits of U.S. workers, and gave Ray Kroc a valuable business opportunity.

The banking business has more than its share of engraved-in-stone, agreed-upon maxims: Employees work short hours and never on Sunday, except for those servicing high-net-worth clients; customers will use ATM machines and the Internet so branches can be closed and tellers let go; customers will tolerate long lines; and coins are to be shunned.

Commerce Bancorp, a Cherry Hill, New Jersey–based retailer of financial services, has run head-on into each assumption, thereby creating a unique brand promise that has propelled it to new heights. In 2003, for example, when deposits for the whole industry rose by just 6 percent, Commerce's deposits were up by 42 percent, to $20.7 billion, and its net income leapt by 34 percent, to $194.3 million. By March 31, 2004, the bank had $25 billion in assets, a 40 percent increase from a year earlier.

Most Commerce branches are open from 7:30 A.M. to 8:00 P.M. on weekdays, but to accommodate early birds and people running late, the bank tacks on an extra ten minutes at each end. In addition, Commerce provides full-service banking for several hours on both Saturday and Sunday. While New York competitors Chase and Citibank were closing branches Commerce was doubling the number of its branch offices. After opening fifty new retail locations in

2004, it will have more than three hundred stores. Customers who prefer to use ATMs are welcome to do so, of course, but Commerce is dedicated to providing every customer with human service.

There are lollipops for customers' children and dog biscuits for their pets. Tellers take turns greeting customers as they enter: "Hi! My name is Karen. How may I help you today?" The bank sends "mystery shoppers" to every branch twice a week, checking to make sure that the service is up to par, the smiles are in place, and the cheery attitudes are genuine. And, to prevent long lines at tellers' windows, Commerce has reduced the number of keystrokes needed for each routine operation: It takes only twenty seconds to verify a signature and cash a check, for example.

Some banks either refuse to accept large quantities of coins or charge extra to count them, which especially irritates business customers making daily deposits. Commerce spent ten million dollars to develop and install Penny Arcades, machines that accept, sort, and count coins by the bucketful, then spool out a receipt for an amount that a teller either deposits directly into the customer's account or exchanges for bills. In 2003, the bank took in $188 million in coins.

Commerce Bancorp is a compelling example of a company that has studied the unchallenged assumptions within its industry, and then crafted a winning, differentiated brand promise by going against the grain.

Or how about Campus Kids, "the weekday sleep-away camps" in Hackettstown, New Jersey; Port Jervis, New York; and Waterbury, Connecticut, that have veered away from the timeworn tradition of keeping campers largely out of touch with their families? The assumption has always been that kids adjust better to camp and suffer a minimum of homesickness if they have no contact with their families other than on visiting days. At Campus Kids the children are away for five days, but then spend weekends with their families.

To be sure, this break from tradition isn't for everyone. However, the arrangement lets working and divorced parents give their children the overnight-camp experience without relinquishing all of their limited together time. It also provides frazzled camp counselors with two days of recovery time each week.

No matter your business, finding a way to break with tradition could be your ticket to a breakaway brand promise.

◆ Rip apart your product assumptions to uncover new brand potential.

You and your colleagues may know everything there is to know about your company's product, but do you know all there is to know about its potential? Do you think about how it could be improved not just in small ways, like a bit more sand in the cement or a touch more red in the packaging, but through significant modifications that would create a unique brand promise? All around you, in numerous companies and industries, managers are looking at familiar products through a new lens and suddenly seeing opportunities that neither they nor their colleagues—nor anyone else in the industry, for that matter—have noticed before.

Take the Schindler Elevator corporation, for instance, a Morristown, New Jersey–based division of Switzerland's Schindler Group. For years the company made high-quality elevators that ran much like those of its rivals': Passengers pressed a button to summon an elevator, then another button to indicate their desired floor. The more people on the elevator, of course, the more stops it had to make and the more impatient everyone became, especially people waiting in the lobby. The aggravation was particularly severe in the many buildings that had neither the space nor the money to add more elevators.

Then Schindler challenged its product assumptions and sparked a breakthrough idea: Passengers approaching a bank of new Schindler elevators see a central control panel on which to key in a floor number. The panel informs its riders which elevator will carry them directly to their floors, then it immediately returns to the lobby to pick up the next customer. This very efficient system moves more people in less time while demanding less space.

Merely signing on to the Schindler Web site exposes a visitor to the company's open, idea-oriented mind-set. There, on the right side of the home page, is the company name atop a vertically moving panel and alongside three vertical red lines. When you click onto another page and scroll up or down the red lines rise or fall independently, always stopping at the same spot on the page—just like an elevator.

Another company that continually examines its product assumptions is the Progressive corporation, an insurance holding company based just outside Cleveland, in Mayfield Village, Ohio. I'll discuss Progressive in much greater detail in Chapter 6, but let me tell you a bit about this innovative insurer right now.

Auto insurance, including property-casualty and liability products, is Progressive's major line of business. The company got its start in 1937 as a mutual insurer. Inventive and successful from the beginning, Progressive really became a contender in 1956, when it began accepting the high-risk clients that other insurers avoided. But even Progressive continued to reject the decidedly accident-prone group of motorcyclists—until, that is, its ongoing customer research turned up an interesting trend that lit a lightbulb in its corporate head.

Although teenage thrill-seekers and macho high-speed rebels were still well represented among motorcycle enthusiasts, Progressive realized that a new and very different group had appeared whose numbers were growing rapidly. Middle-aged professionals in cities around the country had taken up motorcycling, joining touring groups and wheeling around the countryside on weekends. Progressive decided to insure them. Today it covers more motorcyclists than any other corporation, and lays claim to being the only insurer endorsed by the American Motorcyclist Association.

One road to revising your product assumptions is to make a list of every problem reported by customers and then brainstorm solutions. Exclude nothing, even ideas that initially seem impossible. An "impossible" solution may inspire you to find a workable one. Remember: Nothing about your existing product is sacrosanct; reconsider your assumptions regularly. What you discover, and your ideas for improvement, could turn out to be a springboard to a unique new brand promise.

◆ **Look your current target market up and down, and focus on a new group if opportunity beckons.**

Your organization is likely to resist any reconsideration of your current target market. Managers feel more comfortable challenging assumptions about products and the broader industry than contemplating new markets. Your current customers are the axis around which your company spins. The product's design, manufacture, distribution, and marketing all grow from the nature of that chosen market. No wonder managers are reluctant to upset the apple cart.

Still, companies that change course to pursue new target markets can achieve startling success. To be sure, a substantial part of your operation will have to change to accommodate the new market's demands, but if the result is a winning, differentiated brand promise, won't it be worth the effort?

To spur inventive thinking about new markets, consider any customers whose attraction to your current product surprised you, as well as those people whose interests you don't, and never tried to, understand. Then imagine what about your product might prove valuable to each group and how they would use what you offer.

Your research will probably yield some strange, even silly, responses, but that's great. You're thinking outside your usual parameters, which is where a unique new brand promise is likely to be found. A previously unimagined customer group may point you toward a rich new market, or at least direct your thoughts into heretofore untraveled territory.

Laura Alber, president of Pottery Barn, found business inspiration in her own experience as a first-time mother trying to furnish her baby's nursery. Unable to find furniture and accessories that met her standards, Alber developed a business plan to broaden Pottery Barn's brand to include those items. The first issue of the *Pottery Barn Kids* catalog, which appeared in January 1999 (around the same time as Alber's baby), offered everything needed to outfit a child's or infant's bedroom, with, of course, Pottery Barn's reliable quality and—something new—a sense of fun. The first Pottery Barn Kids store opened in September 2000, followed by its Web site in 2001.

As each extension of the original brand met success, Alber raised the stakes. In 2003, when the company dove into a whole new ocean with its *PBteen* catalog, it became the first home-retail chain to stake out this market. And it all happened because Laura Alber had a great idea that, in retrospect, seems obvious. By transforming a lesson from an experience in one part of her life into a breakthrough idea in another, she created a unique brand promise that is simple and straightforward.

Developing a differentiated promise from scratch, as Pottery Barn did, is not the only way to go. Earlier I told you about Cardiac Science's product and brand promise, but let me tell you the story of how it came to pass. Cardiac Science bought its way into competition in September 2001, with the purchase of Survivalink, a Minnetonka, Minnesota–based rival.

After being spun off from Medstone International in 1991, the newly independent Cardiac Science focused on developing its automatic defibrillation device called Powerheart (the company's Nasdaq symbol? DFIB, of course). All through their hospital stays high-risk cardiac patients are hooked up to the Powerheart by electrodes. If a patient arrests Powerheart automatically and instantaneously defibrillates the heart, starting it beating again.

Before Powerheart's introduction Cardiac Science suffered intense financial and technical difficulties, as evidenced by the fact that at the end of 1996 its entire staff consisted of two people. But then Raymond Cohen took over as CEO and gradually got the company on its feet. In January 2000, Powerheart became the world's only automatic external defibrillator (AED) cleared by the U.S. Food and Drug Administration (FDA); thousands of them are now on duty in hospitals around the world.

Once Cardiac Science was out of the woods Cohen focused on broadening the company's brand to encompass a new market for portable equipment. Recognizing that the inpatient market is static, the company looked to a smaller, portable AED that could be used by police, fire, and ambulance services. As part of this initiative Cohen pursued and captured Survivalink, which was already producing AEDs. The FDA cleared the marriage of Cardiac Science's software with Survivalink's hardware in February 2002. Now, the small, user-friendly, and, most important, effective device is being used in myriad locations, from homes to amusement parks.

◆ **Survey your marketing methods and apply a fresh approach where needed.**

Thinking anew about brand targets inevitably sparks fresh ideas for improving your brand presentation. Some years ago executives at GE Plastics, based in Pittsfield, Massachusetts, realized that the company was losing some name recognition. A survey revealed that only 3 percent of the U.S. business managers interviewed could name the General Electric company as a manufacturer of plastic resin.

The poor showing motivated the company to conduct an intense study of its brand's role in the industry; the goal was to determine which aspects of the product and the brand promise differentiated GE Plastics from its rivals. The researchers found that the most important thing the company delivered to its customers was not plastic material, but competitive advantage. In other words, GE Plastics enabled its customers to please their customers.

With new insight, the company drastically altered its marketing approach, essential to the repositioning of its brand promise. Rather than focusing on the various features of its own products the company created an advertising campaign that concentrated on its customers' end products. In each ad, wrapped around the end product—a Volkswagen Beetle, for example—was the line "Sometimes you have to throw the competition a curve to gain an edge." Ads placed in trade magazines, the standard communication vehicle for plastic resin manufacturers, scored a big hit in the industry.

The success of the campaign inspired the company to promote its product directly to the end users. The ads were placed in *BusinessWeek, Fortune,* various design publications, and automotive magazines, with impressive results. A new survey showed that the recognition of GE Plastics among the magazines' readers had soared, with many interviewees naming it as the top supplier of plastic resin.

Challenging marketing assumptions also led to major improvements in how the Whirlpool corporation presents its brand. A probing look at existing programs inspired a totally new addition to the Benton Harbor, Michigan–based company's brand promise: the Insperience Studio.

The Insperience Studio is a collection of fully equipped kitchens in Atlanta, Georgia, where customers can get acquainted, at their leisure, with the latest Whirlpool and KitchenAid home appliances. It was devised to address what the company saw as a major sales problem: "Customers go into a store," David Provost, director of purchase experience, told Scott Kirsner of *Fast Company,* "and they see row upon row of white boxes. They get confused, because everything looks alike. When they talk to a salesperson, they feel as if they end up buying what the salesperson got the best commission on or what was overstocked."

Visitors to the Insperience Studio are guided by a staff person through laundry rooms, patios, and kitchens with appliances that are hooked up and ready to go. The guide can demonstrate, for example, how to program the refrigerated range that keeps food cool for a designated number of hours and then starts to cook it. The studio holds holiday parties and will organize children's birthday parties around food and drink preparation. Visitors are encouraged to try out the equipment for themselves—putting trash in the compactor or baking a loaf of bread.

Neither showroom nor appliance store, the studio exerts no pressure to buy. In fact, no purchases can be made there. The goal is to acquaint customers with the latest products in a way that allows them to fully experience the appliances. Whirlpool describes it on its Insperience Studio Web site as "a studio of solutions and a resource for great ideas"—a place where consumers can visualize having and using the company's products in their own homes, something that is nearly impossible in a conventional store.

Besides answering questions and offering product demonstrations, Whirlpool salespeople gain insight into customers' concerns and learn how to respond to them effectively. Furthermore, the studio is invaluable to company designers, who carefully analyze visitors' interactions with the products.

What is most important about the Whirlpool case, however, is how the company was able to expand its brand promise in a unique way simply by taking an entirely new approach and moving beyond secure marketing parameters.

◆ Rigorously review your business model to make way for an innovative change, of course.

I am continually surprised by companies that simply tweak their business models—rather than conduct a full-scale review—to accommodate changes in their competitive space and the world. Competition is far too brisk for halfhearted tactics. In every industry new business models are bursting on the scene and changing the prospects of every company. Competitors that respond by scurrying to mimic the pioneer inevitably incur costs and lose sales.

There is another option. You can be the one that breaks new ground. You can recast crucial elements of your business model to present a compelling, differentiated brand promise. Of course, that requires fresh thinking and a willingness to entertain unsettling changes in the way you do business.

In the early 1980s Harley-Davidson, the legendary motorcycle manufacturer based in Milwaukee, Wisconsin, bit the bullet and spit it out, thus saving the company. Struggling for more than a decade, twice teetering on the cusp of bankruptcy, its leadership finally decided to revamp the business model by radically overhauling design, production, and the way it presented itself to customers. To ensure that quantity would not compromise quality, Harley reduced the number of bikes it was producing. To retain current customers and attract new ones, it formed the Harley Owners Group (or H.O.G.), with the goal of building a stronger sense of community. It worked; Harley owners turned into Harley boosters, with their own language and traditions.

Altering its business model and strengthening its brand promise shifted Harley into overdrive. When conditions changed again Harley was able to rethink its business model to develop an imaginative, effective, new brand solution. Today Harley-Davidson is a multibillion-dollar company whose sales and earnings just keep going up. In 2003, for example, Harley recorded a 19.9 percent year-over-year rise in sales, to $4.9 billion, while net income jumped 31 percent, to $760.9 million.

I've already told you quite a bit about Samsung. What I haven't said is that it is a turnaround story driven by a studied change in its business model.

In 1997, the company was in deep financial trouble, struggling to compete in the cutthroat market for cheap, copycat microwaves and television sets. Samsung's business model, based on slashing costs, boosting production, and flooding the target marketplace, wasn't working. The company set about reinventing itself as a fast-moving high-end-market pioneer. The foundation of its new business model, as I said earlier, was relentless technological and design innovation.

Samsung products are now cutting-edge. The ruby-red A220 cell phone, for instance, introduced in October of 2003, looks like a cosmetics compact and includes a display that converts into a mirror. Among its other features it suggests appropriate dress, given the day's weather, and offers tips on dieting. The phone sells for a substantial $440 in Korea.

Aside from the company's skill at beating its competitors to market with the latest and best products, Samsung responds with speed and agility to changes in technology or the economy. Chris Dinwoodie, a UBS analyst, called Samsung "a master of makeovers" in *BusinessWeek*. Samsung's ability and willingness to transform its business model means that it sees opportunities where competitors see problems. While its rivals struggle to sidestep a problem, Samsung perceives an occasion to redesign its business model so as to offer customers a fresh, more compelling brand promise. And customers respond: In 2003, Samsung built more than fifty million phones that sold for an average price of $188 outside Korea.

If your company is not as proficient as Samsung at riding the waves of change you, as the company's leader, must become its agent of change. Examine your business model as if you've never seen it before, and revise where needed. Consider what weaknesses you can either strengthen or outsource, and what strengths you can capitalize on. If, for example, your back-office operations are superior to those of rivals, consider offering to become their back-office vendor. Rethink every aspect of your business model.

◆ **Keep it simple and watch a more
substantial brand promise emerge.**

Whether you're changing a specific product, a marketing approach, or a supply chain simplification can powerfully enhance your brand promise.

The Cleveland, Ohio–based Sherwin-Williams company did precisely that when it created a new plastic container for its Dutch Boy Paint, making the inconvenience and aggravation of metal paint cans obsolete. With its twist-off lid and no-drip spout, the "Twist & Pour" simplified an unnecessarily messy and complex process. Customers couldn't get the improved product quickly enough.

The Toyota Motor corporation advanced its brand promise, too, with its justifiably famous just-in-time manufacturing system. By raising product quality while cutting production costs the system enabled Japan-based Toyota to seize a major share of the U.S. automobile market.

Toyota virtually banished manufacturing inventory by demanding that vendors make deliveries as they were needed. Requiring constant, detailed communication between manufacturer and supplier, the new system fostered close, long-term partnerships between the two groups, replacing the traditionally adversarial relationship. At the same time, Toyota's quest for quality led it to give each assembly-line worker the authority to halt the entire line at the first sign of a defective part or faulty assembly. With these steps the company pared away dozens of routine yet unproductive practices and simplified its supply chain.

Saintly patience is almost always required when renting a car at an airport. For no obvious reason, the anachronistic procedure has remained in place amidst extreme competition in the car-rental business. But one savvy competitor, National Car Rental, of Fort Lauderdale, Florida, is making a difference by simplifying the process.

At National you make your reservation by phone or online. Then, when you arrive at the airport, you bypass the National counter and proceed directly to the row of cars in the category you reserved. Within that row you select whatever car you want and drive away.

National's convenient, pared-down approach, called Quickrent, differentiates its brand promise and makes the company an industry pioneer, with all the benefits that implies.

◆ Don't try to go it alone; find a partner and dance.

Legendary marketer Ray Kroc saw the connection immediately, but it took awhile for Disney to warm to the idea. Today any child will tell you now that if their "kid's meal" is not accompanied by a Disney character, fresh from the big screen, it simply doesn't taste as good. Youngsters can collect eight varieties of Brother Bear toys, Pocahontas, and the Littlest Mermaid, while numerous other Disney figures appear on the food chain's napkins, meal boxes, posters, and placemats.

Disney and McDonald's are a winning match. From McDonald's perspective, Disney's characters enliven the dining experience; from Disney's viewpoint, McDonald's is an advertising venue replete with a never-ending stream of children. This is a perfect example of partners doing for each other what each cannot do alone.

A partner can add a new dimension to your brand, including a fresh product line, advanced technology, or unequaled marketing expertise. For example, when catalog merchant Lands' End, of Dodgeville, Wisconsin, was seeking interesting ways to distinguish its Web site, it teamed with WebLine Communications, which had software that allowed Lands' End's call-center representatives to serve customers contacting the company via their computers as well as from their telephones. If a customer calls to say she's having trouble traversing the site the sales rep can actually take control of the customer's browser and navigate it to the desired locations.

Furthermore, the partnership with Burlington, Massachusetts–

based WebLine allows customers and their friends to shop online together. Only the customer who logged on first can make a purchase, but friends can simultaneously view the same items, chat, and offer advice.

Another major retailer that has parlayed its partnership expertise into a powerful brand promise is Target, the upscale discounter. Negotiating exclusive arrangements with some of the world's most famous designers has allowed Target to imitate high-end items with unique, affordable products. Working with the designers is one explanation for the special panache driving its success. Architect Michael Graves, the first of these partners, currently employs two dozen designers who create products for Target, ranging from a fondue set to a toilet bowl brush. A more recent liaison is with fashion and shoe designer Isaac Mizrahi, who designs women's upscale, casual separates priced starting at $9.99 for a ribbed tank or a long-sleeve T-shirt, in contrast to the $20,000 gowns that were once his specialty.

Constantly looking for new kinds of partners, Target has recently teamed with Virgin Group, a British-based conglomerate that focuses on entertainment, music, and travel services. Together they are producing a line of "personal electronics," including telephones, clock radios, and MP3 players. These items, promoted under the name Virgin Pulse, are technologically advanced and easy to use.

Target's willingness to work with partners permits it to refresh and improve its brand promise continually.

Whether or not you consider it appropriate to take on a partner right now, I suggest that you at least briefly consider the possibilities nonetheless. Perhaps the very problems that hamper your company could be resolved by teaming with someone having expertise in your problem area. If you find the right one, a partner can dramatically enhance your brand promise and quickly separate you from the pack.

◆ Open wide the information portals
to increase customer connections.

Needless to say, your company's relationships with customers have to be among your highest priorities; the closer and warmer these connections, the more likely you are to keep their business. The ideal relationship, from your point of view, is one of interdependence and mutual trust.

In recent years more and more companies have encouraged such feelings by offering customers unbiased information about general topics—how to cope with economic change and health problems, for instance, or the scoop about a specific marketplace or a competitor's services and products.

Citigroup's Smith Barney, with headquarters in New York, is one of several brokerages that regularly send clients a newsletter summarizing the state of the financial markets and analyzing near- and long-term prospects, while Whole Foods Markets, based in Austin, Texas, displays health information around its stores. By identifying themselves in customers' minds as reliable, concerned resources, these organizations have profited from differentiating their brands.

Some companies are keeping customers informed to the point of offering the online browser a chance to compare the company's products to those of competitors. Progressive, for example, provides competitive insurance quotes on its home page. By making it easy for customers to comparison shop the company makes clear that it has nothing to hide. The message is: We understand the importance of researching the field, so we'll make it easy for you to do so.

Once word spread that Progressive's Web site offered this feature it became the most popular in the industry and attracted a flood of potential customers. Its willingness to list its competitors' products and rates boosted its credibility. Without doubt, a trusted organization gains a major advantage.

There are many ways you can boost your brand promise by offering customers advice on matters they care about. If your product is in the health-care field you might share medical information with your customers; if you manufacture automotive parts you might take a prominent role in dispensing materials about auto safety. The object is to build trust into your brand identity. Nothing could be more important for your long-run success.

◆ **Confront your fear of new technology,
and embrace brand-building breakthroughs.**

Some companies—3M, Pfizer, and Intel come readily to mind—rely altogether on their scientists to discover the scientific or technological breakthroughs that will differentiate their brands from the opposition. Most organizations, though, lack such extensive in-house resources. They have to stay au courant with technical advances and have the imagination to envision how they might benefit from them. Most likely, your company already has someone who tracks relevant findings and keeps the organization apprised of them. If not, you should correct that shortcoming now. Being the first to incorporate new technology into your product offering almost guarantees an inimitable brand promise.

Once you are informed of the research the next step is to study its importance for your company. Don't reject an idea just because it seems impractical; jot it down along with those that appear more achievable. Let your mind roam over the possibilities. When you finish give the list to a colleague, asking her to repeat the exercise. On any given day your ideas may come to nothing, but the process of mental experimentation will eventually bear fruit. Intuitively associating links among seemingly disparate elements can lead to an imaginative breakthrough.

Suppose you own a mall, and despite the fact that you have tried every kind of directory you can think of, visitors are still having trouble finding the stores they seek. Then you read about the Global Positioning System (GPS), the worldwide radio-navigation satellite system, and discover that the latest models, which use satellites as reference points, can accurately track an item to within a centimeter or so.

You can't help but wonder if a handheld GPS could replace, and vastly improve, the mall's current signage by directing shoppers, say, to jeans on sale or to McDonald's. The devices could be issued to visitors with electronic tags attached that emit a loud signal so as to prevent theft. Talk about a breakthrough brand promise!

At Superquinn, a chain of nineteen supermarkets in and around Dublin, Ireland, new technology has helped the company gain a substantial 8.7 percent share of the nation's grocery business. Customers can consult interactive recipe planners, then scan their items and check themselves out. Superquinn also uses a DNA-tracing technology to assure customers that its meat is safe.

These technological applications were envisioned by a perceptive person at Superquinn who recognized the powerful advantage such differentiation could offer the grocer's brand promise. As you reinvent your brand promise, nothing is more important than your own imagination.

Following the suggestions in this chapter will help you develop a unique brand promise—your overpromise. But an overpromise is nothing without a means of overdelivering it. The most efficient way to do that is to take full advantage of your three TouchPoints, the three primary points of interaction between your company and its customers. Just ahead, in Part 2, I begin with the Product Touch-Point and how you can optimize it to overdeliver your brand promise.

PART TWO
OVERDELIVER

◆

You've developed a fantastic brand promise,
an overpromise. To make the most of it,
you have to supercharge your TouchPoints—
Product, System, and Human.
It's time to overdeliver.

CHAPTER 5

Optimize Your Product TouchPoints

LOVE 'EM OR HATE 'EM, Hummers cannot be ignored, and the people who drive them are passionate about their vehicles. Web sites abound with Hummer clubs, Hummer experiences, Hummer pictures, Hummer accessories. There's even a guy named Ed who's beseeching total strangers from his www.edneedsahummer.com site to send money so he can buy what he apparently believes he can't live without. And whether you're part of the love 'em crowd or someone who prefers the clever anti-Hummer send-up on the Sierra Club's Hummerdinger site, you have to admit that this car/truck/tank lives up to its billing as being "like nothing else." This is the story of a perfect alignment of Product TouchPoint with brand promise.

It was during the first Gulf War that the precursor Humvee rumbled into the public consciousness. Built for rugged, off-road conditions, this clunky military vehicle had high ground clearance and controls for adjusting the tire pressure to every surface from cement to sand. After the war, manufacturer AM General Corporation started selling a slightly modified civilian version, the Hummer, or H1, that offered a stripped-down interior, an uncomfortable ride, and a macho image, all for a mere one hundred thousand dollars. Well-heeled "real men" like Arnold Schwarzenegger bought them, but this was no mass-market vehicle. Only seven hundred a year were sold.

Then the General Motors corporation got into the act, having acquired the Hummer name and marketing and distribution rights from AM General. The year was 1999 and sport utility vehicles (SUVs) had taken the car market by storm. Michael DiGiovanni, a market-research specialist, thought the time was ripe to bring out a smaller, friendlier version of the Hummer. GM's board went along, and the H2 was launched in July 2002. Its brand promise: attention-grabbing machismo with all the comforts.

The H2, though smaller than its predecessor, still weighed in at 3.2 tons. It listed for fifty-four thousand dollars. Yet, in spite of its size and price—or perhaps because of them—it was an instant hit. Within six months the Hummer was outselling the Cadillac Escalade, the Lincoln Navigator, and the rest of the luxury SUV market. Its popularity led dealers to load up their vehicles with extras like chrome wheels and tubular tail-lamp guards (or they simply pushed up the price), so that customers ended up paying more like sixty-four thousand dollars. But that was just fine with the target customer, the object of the Hummer brand promise, an under-sixty urban or suburban male with substantial disposable income and a yearning for a vehicle that would identify him as richer and manlier than anyone around him.

The Hummer perfectly supports the brand promise at the Product TouchPoint. The styling retains the boxy, bulked-up military look of the Humvee, including the oversized, adjustable tires. It comes in look-at-me colors like bright yellow and red metallic. The body is set on a GM pickup truck platform with a V8 engine that provides maneuverability and smoothness of ride comparable to that of other large SUVs, and the Hummer interior pretty much matches them in terms of luxury and comfort. In short, the Hummer is exactly what it promises: attention-grabbing machismo with all the comforts.

Although sales of the H2 began to cool at the end of 2003, GM dealers still moved 35,259 Hummers off the lot over the course of the year despite the sluggish economy and the gathering storm over gas-guzzling SUVs. DiGiovanni and GM were understandably thrilled—but not complacent. They were scheduled to bring out a new pickup truck version, the H2 SUT, in May of 2004, followed by a smaller and cheaper (thirty-thousand-dollar range) sport utility, the H3, in 2005. A Jeep Wrangler–sized H4 is also in the works.

The new focus on smaller and cheaper could not come at a better time, since sharply rising gasoline prices in the first half of 2004 seemed to be accelerating the slowdown in Hummer sales. But whether or not DiGiovanni, now general manager of Hummer, and GM can successfully attract a different breed of customer to a scaled-down product remains an open question. If DiGiovanni truly understands that the Product TouchPoint must be continually monitored and updated to meet changes in customer tastes or the marketplace as a whole, his stated belief that the Hummer brand is still in its infancy and has plenty of room to grow may yet be borne out.

In the pages ahead I offer a number of case histories of companies that have found impressive ways to improve their Product Touch-Points. First, though, let's revisit the concept of TouchPoints in general, what they are and are not, and why they are so important.

TouchPoints are powerful points of contact between you and your customer that help you fulfill your brand promise. If capturing customers is all about your brand promise, keeping that promise is all about how you manage the TouchPoints. We started with the Product TouchPoint because your product is the reason you have a business relationship with customers in the first place.

(To head off any confusion: When I speak of the Product Touch-Point I am referring to service offerings as well as to material goods. A service, after all, is also a product—a product of your company's ingenuity, its systems and processes, and especially of those employees who actually provide it. There are few services today that do not also include tangibles—a report of findings from a consulting service, for instance—and there are few products that don't also include services, such as financing or delivery. For that reason I find it helpful to get everyone thinking in terms of outputs to customers, defined as products.)

The Product TouchPoint occurs when a customer comes into contact with the goods or service you are offering to attract his or her interest—and his or her cash. At that moment your fate is sealed, at least as it relates to this specific product and this particular customer. You rise or fall at the Product TouchPoint. It's love it or leave it. And it's not just a single sale that is at stake. If your company is like most it can't prosper on the basis of one-night stands. Your business relies on customers who come back for your product again and again. To keep them coming you have to stay in tune with their changing needs and wants, while continually modifying the Product TouchPoint to fit. In fact, a static TouchPoint is almost an oxymoron.

Nor does the Product TouchPoint encompass only the actual product or service itself. The TouchPoint also includes the product availability and ease of acquisition. Is there parking near the store? Does the store have the product in stock? In my size? In the color I want? Is the store open at times when I am free to shop? Is there simple, one-click access with easy-to-follow directions if I want to order the product online? The TouchPoint also covers such things as information about the product, competitive offerings, packaging, shipping methods, financing options, warranties, parts-and-service availability, return policies, recyclability, and so on. In other words, the Product TouchPoint takes in all those aspects of interaction with the customer that reinforce or alter his or her expectations about the product.

Remember Betamax? Maybe not, if you're part of the twenty-something crowd. Anyway, with all its advanced features and ease of use, the Sony corporation arguably had the superior video recorder, the better product. But its competitors were focused on building a bigger bank of video titles that customers could play on their VHS systems—and that "side issue" turned out to be the deciding factor in the race. Of course, to customers it was never a side issue at all, which is why doing firsthand research with the real users of your product is so critical when shaping your brand promise.

Apple Computer experienced the same kind of competitive disaster. Even though its personal computer was clearly more user-friendly, customers defined "better" as the availability of software titles. As a result, the Microsoft corporation and the PCs dependent on its multiple software applications inherited the world. Although Apple's epiphany is most likely too late to ever dislodge Microsoft from its perch, the company may have learned its lesson, both in terms of product availability and proprietary systems. Its iPod MP3 player has been a huge success, in part because of the availability of a huge library of songs through iTunes in a safe, easy-to-use, fairly priced format, and both iTunes and iPod products are being built for PC as well as Apple users.

Even though the Product TouchPoint is where your company's brand promise comes to life or dies a lingering death, disconnects between products and promises are all too familiar: stain removers that don't; weight-loss diets that add pounds; magazine articles that fall short of their cover headlines; cell phones that provide poor reception. The list is lengthy.

Some years ago *USA Today* reported that one of every four purchases ends up being a problem for the customer. I believe it.

I once spent a whole day trying to take a test drive during a nationwide promotion of a new car. Of the four dealerships in San Diego, California, two were closed, one was so swamped that no one would talk to me, and the salesman at the fourth literally threw some keys at me and told me to have a good ride. Guess what? I bought another brand. The discrepancy between promise and TouchPoint was just too pronounced.

One little noted reason why the Product TouchPoint deserves special attention is that it gets people talking—for better or worse. I am certain that traditional advertising is no longer the most effective way to build a brand; word of mouth has supplanted it.

In the heady days after World War II advertising was indisputably the most efficient and effective way to build a brand. Goods and services had not been widely available, so there was huge pent-up demand for virtually everything. Television had burst onto the scene, and everyone watched the few available channels. Customers had jobs and money to spend, and television advertising gave them information they needed ("sale next Tuesday") while triggering awareness of new brands and products. But in the intervening years advertising's preeminence has eroded almost as fast as its costs have soared, and today branding is only marginally about advertising. Personal experience with the brand and word of mouth are the new drivers for brand growth. Indeed, they are not only the top two reasons why customers choose a brand; they are also growing in importance relative to other factors. They simply work faster, more effectively, and less expensively than anything else.

Truth is, skyrocketing costs are only part of the reason today's most successful new brands spurn advertising; another is the fragmentation of the media, which has cut into the market share of even the top-rated shows. As a result, you end up paying more while fewer potential customers get to see your product. Worse yet, the public no longer believes your messages. Ads aren't trusted, so readers and viewers simply tune out. Some change channels, some chat or leave the room, and some use TiVo or its imitators to fast-forward.

Even more self-defeating, advertising can actually undermine a brand if the product and corporate structure aren't aligned to deliver its promise. When Oldsmobile, which had traditionally appealed to middle-aged and older customers (who else would be enticed by an *Olds*-mobile?), launched a new, youth-oriented brand promise with the slogan "Not Your Father's Oldsmobile," young buyers were indeed attracted. But when it turned out that the promise was not borne out by the car itself, or by any of its Human or System TouchPoints, the campaign backfired. The entire Oldsmobile division of General Motors has been shuttered.

To be sure, advertising has its uses, particularly in defending and reinforcing an already leading brand. And advertising can certainly be used as part of a strong mix of other marketing tools. But relying solely or even predominantly on advertising to tell your story and differentiate your brand is folly. Today's customer, inundated as he is by the ever-rising tide of television and print ads, has become, in whole or in part, pitchproof. Traditional advertising may help when planning a grand opening or a sale, but it doesn't do much for businesses in the long run.

What really does the job is buzz. Word-of-mouth advertising, besides being free, is what motivates people to try something new. The pitch they ignore when it appears on their television screen becomes a powerful motivator when it comes from a trusted acquaintance. Increasingly, the message is passed along via the Internet, in e-mail messages from friend to friend, relative to relative. You can't beat it for effectiveness.

And just how does the buzz get started? At the Product Touch-Point, where customers get a chance to examine a product or service and react to it—and pass the word.

Now let's get started overdelivering on your overpromise with a look at how five winning companies have gone about optimizing their Product TouchPoints. Each case will highlight a number of ideas that in one form or another might fit your company's needs.

Let's start with the Hummer saga, an unqualified success story replete with valuable lessons for optimizing Product TouchPoints. It represents, as I said before, a perfect alignment of Product TouchPoint with brand promise.

1. Differentiation is in the details. Hummer's designers might easily have gone with traditional colors; instead, they went the extra mile to find vibrant, seldom-used colors that would reflect and support the attention-getting piece of the brand promise by truly distinguishing the Hummer from other vehicles.

2. Cater to customers. It's hard to go wrong accommodating customers' desires for luxury and comfort. On the face of it you might have thought the people attracted to Hummers would be so caught up in the military macho of the vehicle that comfortable seats or a smooth ride would actually turn them off. GM knew better: The target customers for the H2 might buy it for its manly look and associations, but the macho act extends only to outward manifestations. After all, successful, affluent men would see no need to put up with the hard seats and bumpy ride of the H1. And lest we forget, every macho man needs a woman to reinforce his manly self-image. But few women will ride in a vehicle (and maybe won't even let him buy it) unless they like it, too.

3. Pricing cuts both ways. GM understood that there was no advantage in pursuing its normal pricing policy by keeping the Hummer's list price as low as possible. The attention-grabbing macho brand promise included an assurance that the vehicle would not be just another SUV, but a rarity on the road; the high price guaranteed that promise. It reduced the number of people who could afford to buy the H2, and it assured those who could that they were purchasing what was, in effect, a limited edition.

4. Playing it safe can be risky. In many ways, GM showed itself to be a savvy risk taker with the Hummer. From the very beginning the decision to buy the brand and then bring out its own version was a stretch, as were the decisions about style, color, and interior design of the vehicle. The Hummer was like nothing else in the GM stable of vehicles or, for that matter, in the offerings of any of GM's competitors. Playing it safe—keeping

your products similar to those already on the market—is no way to break out of the pack and deliver on a unique brand promise.

Yellow Roadway—"Yes, We Can"

There was a time when customers seemed almost incidental to the business of the Yellow Freight System. Sure, the company had some three hundred thousand of them, and they were paying it $2.5 billion a year to truck heavy freight across the United States and, through a network of partners, around the world. But when a customer called to order a shipment, no one asked when he wanted it delivered. Instead, he or she was given an arrival time that might or might not come true.

What mattered back then was the company's obsession with efficiency. Staffers monitored how much freight was moving, how much fuel was being used, and how full the trailers were. If there was empty space a shipment might be held until more goods showed up. What the customers wanted, the company believed, was speedy delivery and low rates, but since there was no measure of customer satisfaction, no one really knew what customers wanted. When Yellow Freight employees were asked how often goods were damaged, bills were wrong, or shipments picked up or delivered late, they guessed anywhere from 10 percent to 20 percent of the time. But the real defect rate was a whopping 40 percent.

Customers finally got fed up with the inflexible schedules and just plain unreliable performance. "Yellow was never willing to work with me," Timothy Slofkin, purchasing manager for Interprint, a printing company in Clearwater, Florida, told *Fast Company*. Slofkin took Interprint's business elsewhere, as did many other customers. In 1995, Yellow Freight chalked up thirty million dollars in losses and started its second round of layoffs in two years.

That's when Bill Zollars, current chief executive of the combined Yellow Roadway, was recruited. His mandate was to transform Yellow and create a new, customer service–oriented brand promise: real-time control of your shipping process with speedy, cost-effective service from first call to electronic payment. A twenty-four-year veteran of the Eastman Kodak company who had just built the Ryder System's integrated-logistics division into a $1.5 billion business, Zollars found the challenge irresistible. Over the next five years he met it by crafting and nourishing a Product TouchPoint that put Yellow in tune with customers and ensured a pleasing shipping experience.

Recognizing that Yellow's corporate culture had developed over seventy years and could not be changed overnight, Zollars set out on an eighteen-month crusade to convert twenty-five thousand employees to a new way of thinking. He started his days at 6:30 A.M. with the drivers at one of Yellow's more than 375 U.S. terminals, then talked to the dock crew, the office staff, and the sales force. At night, he met with customers, becoming, in effect, a deeply caring, focused, attentive, and evangelistic Human TouchPoint.

Zollars's simple message was a shock to the Yellow system: Stop telling customers "Sorry, we don't do that." The new message would be "Yes, we can." Whatever the customer wanted, Yellow would figure out a way to deliver. It wasn't an easy sell, but the leader's very presence in the system's far-flung outposts was impressive. And after many repetitions, the message sunk in. "We've gone from being a company that thought it was in the trucking business to being one that realizes it's in the service business," Zollars told *Fast Company*.

What that realization means for Yellow's customers is a shipping experience designed to deliver a series of pleasant interactions. First, callers no longer encounter a one-size-fits-all long-haul carrier doing business by its own rigid book. Clients now pick from a variety of services at the Product TouchPoint, including regional shipping, expedited shipping, and customized shipping for small and mid-sized companies. Customers themselves decide whether their freight will be delivered in a week, in several days, or in hours. They can also specify morning or afternoon delivery, or something even more exact. And for expedited orders, Yellow offers a money-back guarantee.

A caller who had previously done business with Yellow now finds that the sales representative already knows the company's location, what type of loading dock it has, the size, weight, contents, and destination of previous shipments, and who signed for past deliveries. If the order is identical to a previous one—say, several thousand pounds of various-sized crates from Chicago to Dallas—the customer can complete the process in about fifteen seconds, less time than it takes to order a hamburger and fries at McDonald's.

Exact Express, Yellow Roadway's quickest, most expensive, and most profitable service, is also its fastest growing. The company's ongoing surveys show that customers want reliable, on-time, and safe delivery of their goods even more than they want low prices. One very tangible indication of how the Product TouchPoint is fulfilling Yellow's brand promise: Exact Express executes perfectly on 98 percent of its expedited, time-definite, guaranteed deliveries. Most customers currently use the service mainly for emergency shipments, but the company sees it becoming a routine part of many just-in-time supply chains.

Companywide, the defect rate has plunged to 5 percent from 40 percent, meaning that 95 percent of all shipments are flawless. Numbers like that go a long way toward changing negative attitudes. Revenues rebounded smartly in 2003 to top $3 billion (a 17 percent gain from 2002), following the dip they took in tandem with the economy. What is more, 2002's $93.9 million pool of red ink turned into a $40.7 million net profit in 2003. And even when business was sluggish the new services continued to grow—a sign of continuing customer happiness. That notion is reinforced by the percentage of customers who say they would recommend Yellow Roadway to friends—it has doubled since 1997.

Yellow's transformed Product TouchPoint is supported by an impressive array of technology. The customer never physically encounters it and may not know it exists, but the information technology—on which the company spends eighty million dollars a year—helps its sales representatives, system operators, drivers, and freight handlers fulfill the brand promise by giving the clients what they want when they want it, and making every interaction a pleasant one.

The profile that pops up on a sales representative's computer screen when a customer calls, for instance, is the product of a smart phone system that recognizes the caller's number and opens the file as the phone begins to ring. Out on the loading docks each employee is equipped with a wireless handheld computer that shows what is on board arriving trucks and where each crate to be loaded is supposed to go. If unloading the pallets takes longer than the system estimates it should the computer gives employees a heads-up.

Yellow's efforts in its lucrative regional delivery business have shortened average delivery times. Some 70 percent of all shipments now take three days or less—a major change from the past. At the heart of this success is the computerized system that lets dispatchers and dock employees schedule the loads with maximum efficiency. Now, shipments to similar destinations can be matched up, thus minimizing the number of times each pallet has to be loaded and unloaded.

The hub of the Yellow Roadway system is the central dispatch office at corporate headquarters in Overland Park, Kansas, a suburb of Kansas City. Like air traffic controllers, the dispatchers view the entire system and every truck in it on a huge electronic map of the United States. Every ten minutes the map updates itself, and the trucks on the road jump to a new location. It gives the dispatchers a high-level view of the day's shipping activity.

Each truck can be displayed with all the shipments it contains—color-coded to show whether they are on schedule—providing the data that enable customers to track their freight online—in real time. In addition, all the drivers in the system can be located and color-coded according to their availability. When the dispatchers spot looming service failures they can work within the web of terminals and drivers to devise solutions.

Each year, Yellow Roadway hosts a conference in Las Vegas for one thousand employees and five hundred customers. Called Transformation, the meeting's message is that the company's changes are far from over. And I agree. Customers evolve, and the Product TouchPoints that make them happy today may be commonplace next week.

Now, let's consider some of the lessons found in Yellow Roadway's transformation of its Product TouchPoint:

1. Make it easy. The customer's convenience often gets short shrift when TouchPoints are being honed. Not at Yellow Roadway. By making all of a customer's previous dealings instantly available to the sales rep who answers the call a repeat order can be taken in a matter of seconds (variations take a little longer). Today's customers, be they businesses or individual consumers, have limited time and are under severe pressure. Speeding them along at the Product TouchPoint can keep them coming back.

2. Make it comfortable. Companies, like people, often feel more comfortable doing things themselves as opposed to relying on suppliers. Why? It gives them a sense of control. Recognizing that concern Yellow relieves the anxieties of customers by making it simple for them to track the progress of their shipments online. Product tracking may not apply to your business, but other ways of easing customer concerns, such as providing long-term warranties or money-back guarantees, can enhance your Product TouchPoint.

3. Use technology in ways that truly matter to customers. Yellow has harnessed technology to deliver information to employees

where and when they need it, not just at call centers but in behind-the-scenes operations. Truck drivers and dock employees are constantly informed about developments affecting their work, thus enabling them to adjust quickly if plans go awry. Getting the word out to your employees in real time can have an enormously positive effect on your Product TouchPoint.

Superquinn—Bringing Them Back

Feargal Quinn, *Fast Company* reports, is Ireland's "pope of customer service." He won that reputation by focusing relentlessly on his brand promise: Every move he makes must be aimed at anticipating and fulfilling customers' every need. The promise is succeeding. Superquinn, Quinn's chain of nineteen supermarkets in and around Dublin, has captured a hefty share of the country's eleven-billion-dollar grocery business. How does Superquinn keep its brand promise? Mainly by constantly tending its Product TouchPoint so that customers enjoy a pleasant and rewarding shopping experience.

Customers walking into a Superquinn are greeted by the tantalizing aroma of baking bread, and when they leave the checkout wait is never more than sixty seconds. If it's raining a complimentary umbrella awaits in a stand by the door. But that's only the beginning of Superquinn's special services and products. How about these:

- Each Superquinn store has a professionally staffed playroom where parents can leave their children while they shop. The care is so good that elementary school teachers in Ireland, a country without preschools, now recognize "Superquinn kids" as exceptionally well prepared for the school experience. Admittedly, the playroom is an expensive feature of Superquinn's Product TouchPoint, but it is also a powerful way of supporting the brand promise and keeps parents coming back.

- Product quality is invariably excellent. Every store has a full-scale bakery, so the bread is never more than four hours old. Twice-daily produce deliveries ensure freshness, a fact that is underscored by the display: Every package of lettuce, mushrooms, or melon is labeled with the date the produce was picked and a picture and biographical sketch of its grower.

- Shoppers don't pay for what they won't use. In a rare example of a cutting-edge Product TouchPoint, scissors are furnished so customers can chop off carrot tops and broccoli and leek stalks before they are weighed.

- Superquinn is dedicated to food safety. This commitment is deeply reassuring to customers concerned about mad cow disease. More than five years ago Superquinn joined with a Trinity College start-up, IdentiGEN, to develop DNA-tracing technology that matches meat with the animal it came from. More than one hundred thousand animals have been tested, which has made customers so confident of the meat's safety that Superquinn's beef sales have chalked up double-digit increases.

- A screen at the checkout counter gives customers a running tab as items are scanned. But when customers get the receipt the items are listed not in the random order of scanning, but by product category. This feature optimizes the Product TouchPoint by making it much easier for customers to decipher and analyze their purchases.

As suggested above, some of Superquinn's magic comes from technology. For instance, the stores are piloting such innovations as self-scan shopping, multifunction kiosks, digital shelf labels, and mobile checkout technology. In addition, the Superquinn in the Dublin suburb of Swords is the world pilot site for the NCR corporation's new retail technology that features futuristic flat-screen displays, kiosks that link customers to their banks, and special services such as wine recommendations and interactive recipe planners.

But technology is important only insofar as it supports the Product TouchPoint and Feargal Quinn's boomerang principle. The big question, he told *Fast Company*, is always the same: "What will this do to help bring the customer back?" And to find the answer he wants his staffers to stay in constant touch with shoppers by actively listening to them and sharing their shopping experience. "If you believe you're in the business of serving the customer better," Quinn says, "then you have to move the center of gravity of the organization to where the business meets the customers."

To remind store managers that their real work is on the shop floor, where the Product TouchPoint occurs and the brand promise is fulfilled or flubbed, the managers' offices are dingy little spaces at the back of the stores. And each month the managers are required to come out from behind the counter and spend time being a Superquinn customer—shopping, asking questions, lodging complaints, and waiting in line. Joining the customer ranks, according to Quinn, quickly teaches employees that what may seem perfectly reasonable and maybe even valuable to the company can be totally off the mark as far as the customer is concerned.

Just as store managers are expected to be out on the floor much of the time, Quinn himself spends most of his week visiting the nineteen stores, chatting with customers, tidying the merchandise, and attending regularly scheduled customer panels or meetings with employees, suppliers, partners, and so forth. He is particularly adamant about one thing: Don't depend on market research or a suggestion box. Talk to customers and actively seek out their complaints.

Quinn learned his management style as a boy, working summers in his father's holiday camp on the coast of County Dublin. He did whatever was needed, from waiting tables to calling bingo games. His father's system was to get full payment in advance and then devote full attention not to maximizing profit from each customer, but to getting customers to book again for next year. If you concentrate on bringing people back again and again profitability will follow, Quinn says. He opened his first shop in 1960, and though he has become an Irish institution through such public-service stints as chairman of the national postal service and a member of the upper house of the Irish parliament, he has been going after the repeat business ever since. What brings the customers back won't necessarily maximize profit—not right away. But Quinn's contention is that repeat business is worth whatever it takes.

Here are some lessons you can take away from the Superquinn saga as you seek to optimize your Product TouchPoint:

1. Every little bit helps. Feargal Quinn wants his stores to cater to customers' concerns and, in his case, that covers a lot of ground that is ignored by the vast majority of retailers. How many markets do you know of that offer an umbrella if it's raining when you're ready to leave, or that not only encourage you to cut off carrot tops before weighing but supply the scissors to do the deed? Those kinds of services won't break the bank, and they'll yield handsome results in supporting your brand promise and developing customer loyalty.

2. Pick your spots and go for broke. At Superquinn, as in your own business, financial constraints apply, but the supermarket throws out the calculator when core products or principles are involved. When mad cow disease first appeared Feargal Quinn did not ignore or pooh-pooh the danger as rival markets did. Instead, he invested substantial sums to make sure the meat his stores sold would be free of the disease. In other words, he approached the problem head-on, taking decisive and costly action to protect an invaluable Product TouchPoint.

3. It's everyone's job. Service at Superquinn is not the exclusive domain of the hourly employees. Managers are expected to

spend most of their time on the frontlines, whether actively helping customers or posing as one themselves at other stores; they sample employee responses to questions and complaints to make sure that the company's service mandates are being followed. Quinn himself spends a large part of his time doing the same thing. The Product TouchPoint is too important not to engage the time and energy of all your people.

4. Trust leads to dollars. Superquinn wants its customers' trust along with their money. In fact, it sees the development of one as the surest, long-term route to the other. So the company removes candy displays at its checkout counters (to save parents from the taunting and tantrums of their children) and makes sure the people who operate its store playrooms are true professionals. If you want to see your brand promise fulfilled, put civility and customer trust above money at your Product Touch-Point.

Tadpole—Powerful Notebooks at a Bargain Price

On the face of it the timing seemed strange, even foolhardy. In 2002, Mark Johnston worked for a British company called Tadpole, which manufactured high-performance notebooks based on Sun Microsystems's Solaris operating system. The company was in trouble, not just because the bottom had fallen out of the computer market and the Solaris system was increasingly losing favor, but because the Tadpole product had a sky-high price tag of twenty thousand dollars. Undaunted, Johnston bought Tadpole for $11.6 million, a sum equal to half the company's notebook sales that year, and set up shop in Cupertino, California.

Johnston envisioned a substantial market for powerful notebooks among engineers who take on major design projects like those involving cars or semiconductors. These engineers rely on computer-aided software that requires far more memory and much tougher microprocessors than typical notebooks can comfortably handle. But unless they are employed by government agencies willing to pony up twenty thousand dollars, these professionals are basically chained to huge Sun workstations in their offices.

Mark Johnston set out to rescue them with a new and compelling brand promise: freedom. Engineers previously tethered to their desks and desktop computers would now have access to 64-bit notebooks weighing in at a mere seven pounds that could do the work of the older, clunkier machines—and at an affordable price.

Fulfilling that promise at the Product TouchPoint turned out to be a tough assignment, even though Johnston was well-positioned to make it happen. Born in New Zealand in 1955, he started out selling Apple and Commodore PCs and went on to found three companies that were engaged in extending the reach and life cycles of Sun Microsystems solutions—all this before he arrived at Tadpole.

To bring the price of his machines—called Sparcles, because they use Sun's Sparc processors—down to $3,000, Johnston ditched the earlier $2,500 liquid-crystal-display (LCD) screens and substituted $300 screens of the type used by Dell. Given that the new notebooks were intended for private—not government—customers, other original design elements were also scrapped. Instead of incorporating two removable disk drives and two Ethernet connections, for example, he provided one of each. And in order to shrink the machine to true notebook size Johnston had to devise advanced cooling techniques that involved work on heat-pipe technology and forced-air cooling.

The resulting product has the outward appearance of a standard consumer notebook. "Our model is to look as much like Dell as possible," Johnston told *Forbes*. The innards, though, are very different and are capable of processing 4-gigabyte data files. Databases, digital videos, and photos can be brought up ten times faster than is possible with traditional notebooks.

Whether Johnston's gamble will pay off remains to be seen. But there are positive signs that the company's Product TouchPoint is fulfilling its brand promise. At Nokia's operations in Carlsbad, California, for example, Tadpole is enabling Bill R. Hall, systems administrator, to avoid having to lease a new building to house some 240 additional software engineers the company has hired. Instead, the new hires are taking turns working at the office and at home on their Sparcles.

Here are some Product TouchPoint lessons to be drawn from the Tadpole story:

1. Know your niche. Mark Johnston made his bid to supply private engineers with the Sparcle based on his intimate knowledge of the territory. He knew that portability was a coveted feature, but he also understood both the size of his target market and the risks involved in pursuing it. Remember: Before you can accurately design your Product TouchPoint you must have an insider's understanding of your would-be customers.

2. Aim your firepower where it can have the strongest effect. Tadpole's unique brand promise of freedom for engineers included a number of elements, but two were at the heart of it: price and size. The company would aim to deliver a machine that weighed less than its predecessors and, just as important, was much cheaper. Tadpole was able to deliver on that promise at the Product TouchPoint by focusing its research and design efforts on those two key goals.

3. Appearance counts. Many a worthy product has bitten the dust because its makers ignored the visual impression it made on customers. And that applies in business-to-business dealings as much as it does in the retail realm. Mark Johnston understood that his potential engineer customers would be impressed at the Product TouchPoint by a machine similar in size and general appearance to a Dell notebook but with all the power of their Sun office desktops.

Chico's—a High-Wire Act

The narrower a company's target market the more it must be committed to a delicate kind of balancing act. Any time it strays from its precisely defined brand promise at the Product TouchPoint it confronts the distinct possibility of falling on its keister. That is the perilous path taken by Chico's FAS, a Fort Myers, Florida–based women's clothing chain. But, as of this writing, it has kept its balance admirably while setting records in terms of both growth and profitability. In fact, Chico's showing for the fourth quarter and year ended January 31, 2004, was astonishing: Its overall sales jumped 56 percent in the quarter and same-store sales were up 21 percent. For the full year, net income skyrocketed 50 percent, to a record one hundred million dollars on a 45 percent gain in total sales.

Chico's clothes are meticulously designed to appeal to baby boomers who have incomes of one hundred thousand dollars or more, are generally more full-figured, and want clothes that are fashionably trendy without being too noisy. The store's brand promise: Our clothing will keep you both stylish and comfortable. And that is just what's delivered at the Product TouchPoint.

Part of Chico's formula is the freshness of its offerings. Every month the whole mix of items changes, and new clothes are added to that mix weekly, even daily. Chico's customers thus pay unusually frequent visits in the course of a year, knowing that there will always be something new and different for them to try on.

Mix-and-match clothing is also important to Chico's Product Touchpoint. "We really take a whole wardrobing approach," Pat Murphy, senior vice president and general merchandise manager, told *Women's Wear Daily*. "We encourage our customer to think in terms of what to wear with what." Not only does the store gather its serious clothing collection with wardrobing in mind, it also carries a range of lesser items that can give an ensemble a different look. These include layering pieces and T-shirts as well as matching, moderately priced accessories like necklaces, bracelets, and watches. All of these products are chosen to support salespeople who coordinate whole new outfits for their customers.

Murphy describes the store's target customer to *WWD:* "She travels a lot, is very active, but doesn't want to look old. She's very pulled together, but in a hurry." She prides herself, Murphy adds, on appearing trendy but not foolish. Chico's travelers collection, for example, features synthetic blends that perform well right out of a suitcase, while its C-Wear collection is made of soft cotton for wearing around the house.

One of Chico's ingenious innovations is its sizing; rather than the usual 4, 6, 8, 10, 12 sequence, the store has just four size categories: zero (traditional sizes 4 to 6) to three (traditional sizes 14 to 16). In addition to making customers feel slimmer, the reduced number of sizes represents a major cost savings for the company. Finding ways to strengthen its performance at the Product Touch-Point is a Chico's specialty.

Now let's consider some general lessons we can draw from that performance:

1. Keep 'em coming. Too often, I think, we tend to work hard at finding a product that will satisfy enough customers. Then we relax and enjoy our temporary success—for it almost certainly will be only temporary. Customers are more demanding and changeable than ever, particularly given the increased comparison shopping potential of the Internet, and you can't expect to keep them for long with the same old fare. Chico's has confronted that problem with a constant infusion of new clothing styles and designs. You may not have to maintain the same frequency, but you would be well advised to keep your offerings fresh if you want to keep fulfilling your brand promise at the Product TouchPoint.

2. Think big. It would have been easy for Chico's to cater to its middle-class, baby-boomer customers with a variety of outfits geared to their needs. But the store's leaders were not satisfied with such a modest goal. They wanted to supply not just an occasional article of clothing, but their customers' entire wardrobes. That kind of big-time thinking may be just what your company needs to achieve greater traction at the Product TouchPoint. Let your imagination loose on the possibilities.

3. Think small. In many clothing stores accessories are viewed simply as low-traffic, high-margin items that can sometimes be piggybacked onto the purchase of a dress or suit. Chico's looks at accessories not as a short-term opportunity but as a major piece of its wardrobing strategy, a key element of its Product TouchPoint. The store saw how a coordinated bracelet or watch could entice a customer to buy a whole top-to-toe outfit, and to support that goal it priced its accessories on the low side. You are almost always going to win by trading a large markup on a minor product for increased sales of your major product.

4. Put mind over matter. Having a superior product or service is never enough. What you have to control, to the best of your ability, is the mental state of the customer at the Product TouchPoint, and that in turn may be a function of the lighting in the sales environment and the attitude of the salespeople. Chico's does its best to elevate that mental state with such standard devices as pleasant surroundings and an amiable sales staff. But it never stops searching for other, more clearly differentiated approaches. Its unorthodox sizing strategy, which assigns customers much smaller sizes than they encounter in other shops, is an example. If you try to emulate Chico's, you will discover that unique solutions may be, like the sizing, astoundingly simple. But you still have to work at finding them.

Samsung—First to Market

Korean electronics juggernaut Samsung has transformed itself from a maker of a slew of low-priced, copycat products into a high-tech powerhouse with a mightily ambitious brand promise: In design and technology we deliver the latest and the best. Yet, at the Product TouchPoint, the company consistently fulfills that promise.

How? For one thing, it is fast. In April 2002, for example, Samsung brought together eighty designers and engineers from its memory chip, telecom, display, computing, and manufacturing arms to work on a new camera phone to be marketed by T-Mobile, the cell phone carrier. It took the team four months to come up with a prototype for the V205, which transmits photographs wirelessly. Thirty Samsung engineers were flown to Seattle, where the new phone was tested on T-Mobile's networks. In November, the V205 was on the assembly line in Korea. And that eight-month leap from idea to finished product was relatively slow for Samsung, where the time from new product idea to manufacture averages five months.

What such lightning speed gives the company is the ability to be first to market with the hottest new electronics gadgets, thereby capturing its target audience of with-it young consumers around the world who want only the very latest. "In the analog era, it was difficult for a latecomer to catch up," Vice Chairman Jong Yong Yun told *BusinessWeek* in 2003, but in the digital era, "if you are two months late, you're dead."

Samsung provides customers with a lot to choose from at the Product TouchPoint, including cell phones, television sets, digital music players, and computer displays. In 2003 alone the company introduced ninety-five new products to the U.S. consumer market. What characterizes these items, aside from their freshness, is the high quality of their design and engineering—an amazing contrast with the goods produced by Samsung as recently as 1997. In 2002, the company's digital appliances actually won five industrial design excellence awards, a feat matched only by Apple.

There are 350 people in Samsung's design operation today, twice the number in the nineties, and they are a far cry from their colleagues in the other departments of what remains, at heart, a most conservative organization. The designers dye their hair the colors of the rainbow and work in jeans and sneakers, but that doesn't seem to alter their serious focus on innovative products, nor lessen their ability to work with their counterparts in more buttoned-up areas. On any given project Samsung insists on intense collaboration among designers, engineers, consumer research specialists, and manufacturing people.

Some measure of their success can be seen in the products themselves, and in their acceptance at the Product TouchPoint. There is a digital phone that lets you watch thirty minutes of video as well as live television, and another that is voice activated. There is a whole line of high-definition TVs using digital light processing technology that have become the best-selling products in the three-thousand-dollar-and-up price range. There is the zippy Yepp digital music player that in just a few years has taken over third place in that booming market.

One advantage Samsung's people have over most rivals is the relative flatness of the organizational structure. It takes fewer signatures from fewer levels of bureaucracy for an idea to gain approval. That not only hastens a product's rush to market but also allows for more risk-taking, breakthrough products.

At the same time Samsung is not wedded to in-house solutions in its demand for excellence. It doesn't hesitate to look to other companies, and frequently pits one of its own teams against an outside team to get the best from both sources. For example, the company gets half of its color filters for the LCD business from within its ranks and the other half from the Sumitomo Chemical company of Japan, and it challenges the two parties to outdo each other.

The consumer electronics business encompasses special demands, but there are some general lessons for improving your Product TouchPoint that can be drawn from the Samsung story.

1. Get there first. Your business may not demand the kind of speed to market that is necessary for a Samsung or a Sony. You may even specialize in piggybacking on product pioneers. But in any case you will want to cut your development time (even piggybackers have competition). A flat organizational structure like Samsung's can save you weeks and even months of battling through layers of bureaucracy to get an item moving toward the Product TouchPoint.

2. Get hot designers. Samsung, traditionally a bastion of Korea's conservative business community, shed those constrictions in hiring its design staff. It didn't matter whether their hair was red or green, or whether they had funny little toys and gadgets on their desks. What mattered was results. When the fate of the company is in the hands of your designers, you should not be unduly concerned about appearance or lifestyle differences.

3. Get everyone involved. Samsung's emphasis on collaboration, on tapping the expertise of all relevant elements of the organization in product development, is worth emulating. It cuts development time because you catch problems sooner and avoid last-minute surprises from the production engineers. Collaboration also contributes to product quality by bringing the best and brightest together to focus on a particular project. The result: a Product TouchPoint that powerfully supports the brand promise.

4. Get them competing. For those aspects of your operation that are absolutely critical to a Product TouchPoint that supports the brand promise you might consider Samsung's ultimate weapon: pitting inside departments against outside vendors. Nothing cuts costs and increases quality like a little competition.

What's Next

Clearly, there is no one formula for creating Product TouchPoints that will enable your company to consistently overdeliver on its brand promise, benefiting both your customers and your cash flow. But after reading this chapter you should have some general principles to guide you in devising Product TouchPoints that fit your unique circumstances.

Although Product TouchPoints are essential to your success—your product or service is the proximate cause, after all, of any contact between your company and its customers—there are other significant TouchPoints that demand your attention. In the chapter that follows I discuss how you can tune your System TouchPoint—your Internet and telephonic points of contact, for example—to reinforce your brand's uniqueness. The goal: to make them so easy to use that most of your customers will prefer this most cost-effective way of doing business with you.

CHAPTER 6

Optimize Your System TouchPoints

AMERICAN EXPRESS has a happy customer named K. Forsthoefel. Why? Because the company has given her a set of System Touch-Points that make her feel cared for and special. Ms. Forsthoefel's story is a fine example of a differentiating brand promise fulfilled.

New York–based financial-services behemoth American Express ($3 billion of profits in 2003 on $25.87 billion of revenues) has recently been customizing its Blue card with offers tailored for different segments of its customers, such as "Blue for Business" and "Blue for Students." Forsthoefel owns a "Blue for Music" card, and her experience with it is proudly posted on the Amex Web site.

> This summer my teenage son was begging me to take him to see his favorite music group play in concert. The band was Creed. I finally gave in and purchased tickets online, using Blue. Much to our surprise they sent us a free CD of the artist we purchased tickets for.
>
> Well, the day finally arrived to go to the show. The ticket confirmation Web page instructed us to go to the Blue will-call window. As we approached the venue, we were all taken aback by the huge crowd waiting to enter. We then easily found the Blue will-call window, and it had only one person in line. Two minutes later, we had our tickets in hand and were headed to the back of the long lines waiting to enter. I have always hated lines with a passion.

Then the lady at the window instructed us to proceed to the Blue entrance. There it was—a special entrance just for Cardmembers with Blue, and to all our delight, no lines!!! We just walked right up, showed our tickets and Blue, and we were in. We had successfully bypassed all lines. Everyone with me was thoroughly impressed.

Many companies might well have considered the easy online purchase and the complimentary CD more than enough to deliver on Blue's brand promise to enhance the customer's musical experience. Amex saw it differently. If the company was to live up to its promise it would have to keep raising the bar, constantly extending and improving the way it interacted with its Blue cardholders.

Extraordinarily successful companies like Amex understand that a good brand promise is built into the entire business and is supported and reinforced by a series of TouchPoints. In the case of customer Forsthoefel and the Blue card, Amex enhanced its Product TouchPoint—the line of credit the Blue card represents—by creating a System TouchPoint that immediately attracts attention and makes its holder feel special because of the bold-looking, graphically arresting iridescent blue square superimposed on the card. But this System TouchPoint's appeal extends far beyond the visual. The Blue card is also a smart card with an embedded chip that identifies the customer and makes the card, as Amex notes on its Web site, "a passport to a whole new music experience." Only Blue music cardholders are entitled to receive a 30 percent discount on recordings by certain musicians at all Virgin megastores, exclusive MP3 downloads from a Blue Web site, and the Summer Concerts in Blue that drew the Forsthoefels to one of twenty-six SFX Entertainment amphitheaters across the country—not to mention that free CD for buying tickets online.

But Amex didn't stop there. It put together a cascade of compelling System TouchPoints—from easy pickup of tickets at the box office and the line-skipping arrangements, to Blue-only listening stands and bin cards in Virgin megastores. The combination of Product and System TouchPoints, supported by the grace note of the Human TouchPoint at the box-office window, fulfilled the card's brand promise—and made customer Forsthoefel very happy.

Understanding the System TouchPoint

A System TouchPoint, as you know, is defined as any point of contact between a company and its customers that does not involve direct interaction with the company's product or its people. That may mean something tangible like a paper shipping form or a plastic prepaid phone card or the Amex Blue card's eye-catching design. These days, technology-related System TouchPoints are enabling dozens of winning companies to overdeliver on their brand promises. Examples abound, from the automated phone system through which subscribers can temporarily stop and restart newspaper delivery without ever speaking to a human representative, to the E-ZPass toll-collection systems in use on numerous eastern highways and bridges. For baseball fans a System TouchPoint makes it possible to order food items and have them delivered directly to your seat.

Enjoying hot dogs, peanuts, popcorn, and the like is part of the fun of going to the game—unless, of course, you're standing in a concession line when a home-team slugger hits the ball out of the park and puts your team ahead. But if you're lucky enough to be in one of the growing number of baseball stadiums that allow you to use your cell phone to have food delivered to your seat, you'll neither starve nor miss the game's most exciting moments.

Twelve of the country's minor-league parks now allow fans to register their names, addresses, and credit-card numbers with a call center. Then, when hunger strikes at the game, they dial the call center, type in their seat number, and order items from the menu they picked up earlier at the gate. The food arrives in about ten minutes. Two major league teams, the Seattle Mariners and the Atlanta Braves, offer variations on the service. This System Touch-Point between fans and the ballpark concessions begins the moment the park's technology interacts with the customer's own cell phone technology.

Like all of my TouchPoints, the System TouchPoint is a moment of truth for a business, an opportunity to fulfill its distinctive brand promise. Doing so successfully requires the System TouchPoint to deliver a simple, convenient, and trouble-free transaction. Additionally, it must meet two important criteria central to my thesis: consistency and scalability.

I cannot overemphasize that your TouchPoints must reliably provide customers with a product, service, or experience they can count on. In addition, if your TouchPoints are to be effective they must be accessible to your customers en masse—that is, they must easily accommodate additional demand as your market expands, which is the definition of scalability. Otherwise, your TouchPoints will fail to do their job of fulfilling your differentiating brand promise. Most important, you will have lost the trust of your customers.

Not only do System TouchPoints help bring consistency and scalability to all your TouchPoints, they frequently offer customers the increasingly popular self-service option. Whether it's pumping gas, withdrawing cash, shopping via the Internet, or paying for groceries, self-service technology allows any number of customers to transact business when they choose and with little or no wait.

At the high end self-service checkout technology can be amazing. In the Boston area, for example, the Stop & Shop supermarket chain offers the Shopping Buddy, a computer that sits on a shelf of the shopping cart. Developed by Cuesol, a privately held company in Quincy, Massachusetts, this System TouchPoint is linked to a wireless network by infrared beacons in a store's ceiling. A shopper picks up her cart by swiping her Stop & Shop loyalty card at a kiosk.

The system tracks the cart's location in the store and offers the shopper special bargains keyed to her whereabouts and her personal shopping history. It also helps her find specific items. She scans each one, drops it into a bag on her cart, and never has to empty the bag or the cart. She turns in her Shopping Buddy, signs the credit-card form, picks up her itemized receipt, and takes the cart to the parking lot.

At the low end, self-checkout technology goes back a decade or more. The FastLane system marketed by National Cash Register, for example, melds a scanner, a scale, a touch screen, a cash accepter/dispenser, and a credit-card reader, none of them revolutionary by today's standards. But the stations sell for just twenty to thirty thousand dollars each, and promise big cost savings as well as improved customer shopping experiences. Self-checkout stations, which are now used in 25 percent of the nation's supermarkets, take up a quarter of the space required by conventional checkout counters, and a single worker can keep an eye on four to six stations.

Whether high-end or relatively low, technology pays off when managers learn to see it as a System TouchPoint that helps them keep their brand promise. But typically it takes years or even decades for new technology to be accepted in its starring role as a System TouchPoint. When automatic teller machines first appeared in the early 1970s banks failed to grasp their true potential. Missing the point that around-the-clock accessibility is an ATM's biggest asset, banks kept the machines in their lobbies, where customers still preferred to do business with live tellers. It took years to teach bank customers that ATMs were faster and more convenient, and then to install the machines in remote locations and make them a revenue source by charging for their services.

Self-service at filling stations took even longer to catch on, and its full potential as a System TouchPoint has yet to be exploited. As far back as the late 1940s, a few stations tried self-service, but conventional industry wisdom held that customers, particularly women, wouldn't pump their own gas. Nevertheless, the practice spread, helped along by the lower per-gallon prices at pumps marked SELF. In the 1980s, "pay at the pump" arrived, with technology at the System TouchPoint that allowed customers to use their credit cards without ever entering the station. Gasoline companies were wary, fearing they would lose the revenues from sales of coffee, chewing gum, and cigarettes that provide a large share of service-station profits. In the end, it turned out that inside sales actually rose because shorter lines at the cash register attracted more customers.

In the mid-1990s, Mobil adapted radio frequency identification (RFID) technology (a World War II innovation to identify friendly planes on radar) to improve its at-the-pump TouchPoint. Mobil put an RFID chip into a small tag for attachment to a customer's key chain. Called Speedpass, this revamped System TouchPoint allowed customers to pay for gas simply by waving their keys at the pump, slicing half a minute off the typical 3.5 minutes it takes to get gas with a credit card. Speedpass is also used at some McDonald's outlets in the Chicago area and at some Boston-area Stop & Shop stores. Meanwhile, ExxonMobil is negotiating to let customers pay with a wave of their keys at other venues, and Wal-Mart is requiring that its top one hundred suppliers be RFID compliant by 2005.

TouchPoints or TorturePoints?

Despite these shining examples of companies successfully using System TouchPoints to deliver on their brand promises, there is a major caveat: Such efforts can, and often do, go terribly wrong. And when they backfire more customers are likely to be turned off to your brand than were ever turned on.

In extreme cases, businesses are turning System TouchPoints into "TorturePoints" for their customers. Customers get disgusted when companies design their technology from their own points of view rather than from those of their paying customers. Such missteps are made mainly to control inventory, prevent fraud, or reduce costs. And living up to the brand promise, if it is remembered at all, is far down the list of priorities. So when System TouchPoints go awry, it's hardly surprising that angry customers come away feeling their needs don't much matter.

Credit-card systems, for example, though supposedly intended to simplify the process of paying for purchases, can actually complicate it. Who hasn't fretted on a checkout line as the system toils to recognize another customer's card and churn out a receipt, which the customer then has to sign. And when you present your card directly to a merchant she may ask to see your driver's license to compare signatures or to compare the picture on the license to the person in the flesh. Any or all of this can—and often does—happen each time you visit this merchant. It's for your own protection, the merchant hastens to explain, but you know full well that the rigmarole is really for the protection of the merchant and the credit-card issuer.

Similarly, most of us have, at one time or another, been infuriated by voicemail systems designed to ensure that you never speak to a live person. Robots with maddeningly chipper voices can understand clearly enunciated spoken words and handle routine transactions fairly efficiently. But if your question is complex or doesn't fit into one of the robot's pigeonholes, you're out of luck. If you persist long enough through one level of automated response after another you may eventually hear a human voice—or, just as likely, you will be cut off. Those in the know can punch in escape codes to bypass voicemail systems and reach an actual person. (The *Wall Street Journal* recently published two dozen such codes, most of which were promptly changed once the word got out.) At Visa, for instance, you could call the customer-service number, 800-847-2911, press zero two times, hang on despite hearing a message that the response is invalid, and finally get connected. For a few lucky customers the gratification was probably intense—at least initially. The real question is why customers were put through such an ordeal in the first place? Any savings in wages for human operators is surely more than offset by the costs of customer frustration and fury.

The technology underlying these System TouchPoints is not being used to fulfill a unique, differentiating brand promise. It is technology gone astray, and it benefits no one other than the people who set it up. It goes without saying that the message to customers is anything but welcoming.

I had an equally, if not more, frustrating experience with a System TouchPoint when I tried to open an Internet banking account online. After entering all the requested information except for the PIN number, which I obviously didn't have at that point, my application was rejected for just that catch-22 reason. When I called the bank's Internet-banking department I was told that I needed to call another number to ask to have my PIN created, wait until it arrived in the mail, and then call back to the first number to apply for the account. This is a System TouchPoint designed for nothing but failure. And making it flatly impossible to open an online account online raises the question of whether there is, in fact, even an online account to be had!

System TouchPoints that go wrong often represent outdated, halfhearted attempts applied over months or years to correct various problems. If they initially provided customers with speedy, consistent fulfillment of the brand promise and allowed for scalability they no longer meet these critical requirements. I suspect that my online-banking TouchPoint, for instance, once worked perfectly well, but was changed without sufficient thought when someone objected that its PIN provision wasn't secure.

Such misguided technology or processes can quickly turn a customer's excitement about a product or service into exasperation. Web sites drive customers away if they don't offer, among other things, a simple but comprehensive home page, phone and fax numbers, e-mail and physical addresses, or other obvious contact information; a way to revert to the previous screen; the option to buy more than one of an item; a search engine; a way to compare similar products from obvious competitors; a link to purchase the item online once you've located it; and a way to prevent having to enter the same information multiple times.

Besides the obviously counterproductive System TouchPoints noted in the previous examples, a marketing approach that has gained some currency bears mention here. It is the idea that every differentiating brand feature must be a compelling experience, a memorable event that will make customers want to pay a premium for your product or service. In other words, music must play and angels must sing at every single product or service transaction in a human's life.

I don't dispute that Product and Human TouchPoints might sometimes benefit from the show-stopper approach, but I am certain that not every TouchPoint in your arsenal, and particularly not the System TouchPoints, needs to play a starring role. Apart from the impracticality of trying to lift every customer encounter to dramatic heights, I don't think it's wise to do it. In fact, some products and situations of use become more difficult to access and inefficient when they get the star treatment—the theater involved actually becomes an impediment to a fast or convenient or satisfying transaction.

It's good to remember that sometimes speed is everything; sometimes silence is golden. Sometimes anonymity is preferred because we just don't have the emotional energy to interact with another human being. Sometimes we want to hem and haw and compare our options without ever-attentive service personnel lurking over our shoulder, or waiting patiently on the other end of the line. In these cases nonhuman service is better service, not a shirking of the service responsibility.

TouchPoint Branding provides a more holistic, wide-ranging,

and balanced approach that uses all the TouchPoints to keep a differentiated brand promise. Thus, when designing your Touch-Points resist any urge to make each and every one a "Wow!" Use your judgment to determine which ones work best when they're little noticed or even completely invisible.

Now, let's look at a few examples of companies that are optimizing their System TouchPoints, and in doing so are supporting and enhancing their brand promises. Each case contains valuable lessons to help you use System TouchPoints to your best advantage.

Sumerset Houseboats—Selling a Lifestyle

With a population of almost twelve thousand, you might think that the landlocked town of Somerset, Kentucky, is a less than ideal place to build half-million-dollar houseboats. That is, until you learn that the Ohio River flows just to the north, the Mississippi runs to the west, and the lakes and reservoirs of the Tennessee Valley Authority are situated to the south and east. Turns out that it's a great location for Sumerset Houseboats (yes, it's Sumerset with a "u").

The company's success is due, in part, to former CEO Thomas Neckel Sr.'s decision to create a new System TouchPoint, a Web site that turned Sumerset's customers into an extended family. (Neckel, who purchased Sumerset in 1997, sold the forty-year-old company to an investment team last year.) The site's central feature is a series of digital photos of houseboats under construction. Changed daily, the photos allow buyers to keep up with each step of their boats' construction, no matter where they live. By closely linking the customers to the company the Web site reflects and extends Sumerset's unique brand promise, which isn't about boats so much as lifestyle. Or, as Cecil Helton Jr., the site's creator, once put it: The boats are just "a hideaway that lets customers . . . capture time with their friends and family."

Initially, Neckel conceived the site as a display for prospective customers to view design options and receive customized information. But then he had an epiphany: Most anyone building a new home likes to keep tabs on the progress. Wouldn't the same apply to a floating home? That's how Neckel came up with the idea that has done so much to improve customer satisfaction.

At first, Neckel thought he would protect his customers' privacy by requiring a password to enter the site. But buyers wanted to see each other's boats to get new design ideas. In a clever compromise Neckel satisfied everyone by making the photos publicly accessible while identifying them with numbers instead of owners' names. Launched early in 1999, the site gets more than forty thousand hits a day, compared to two hundred hits a week for the static Web catalog it replaced.

Besides its obvious popularity with Sumerset's current and potential customers, this System TouchPoint had serendipitous effects as well. For one thing, Neckel said, Sumerset's employees became more productive. It seems that knowing their works-in-progress were being observed by customers made employees want to be seen as moving steadily forward. Another invaluable side effect: the almost immediate discovery of errors. For example, when Sumerset's workers began installing the wrong entertainment center in a boat under construction the customer caught the mistake before it turned into a costly problem. "Two weeks later, it would have been major dollars to fix," said Cecil Helton in an *Inc.* magazine article. Then, too, allowing buyers to monitor their boats' progress online saves time and money that the company once spent on entertaining customers, who typically made six or seven visits to the plant during the construction process. Follow-up visits have been reduced to a minimum. All in all, this System TouchPoint has yielded handsome returns for Sumerset: quality control, cost reduction, and increased productivity, not to mention happier customers.

And customers are delighted with this TouchPoint. Debra and Bruce Wollaber, who ordered a three-bedroom, two-bath houseboat a few years ago, logged on daily to follow its construction. On the first day the gleaming aluminum hull of boat no. 2891 was completed, after which the Wollabers saw the deck being laid, machinery being installed, the superstructure being framed, and the kitchen and entertainment center put in. After six weeks the finished 18-by-86-foot craft set off on a one-day test cruise on the company pond. Initially frightened by the thought of designing a houseboat, Debra found the process "totally enjoyable," due in no small part to the excitement of watching her boat being built from the hull up. As she told *Inc.*, "One day I asked for pictures of a specific part of the boat, and [they were] posted . . . the next day."

Besides showcasing the custom houseboats it builds and glowing testimonials from satisfied customers, Sumerset's site also operates as a clearinghouse for people buying and selling used houseboats. (On the day I visited the site the used-houseboat offerings ranged from a small, $49,000 boat built by another manufacturer to a larger, $399,000 Sumerset creation.) In fact, what Sumerset has done is to use its unique System TouchPoint to create a houseboating community similar to H.O.G. (Harley Owners Group), the enormously successful motorcycling community Harley-Davidson created with its Web site. As such, Sumerset's bulletin board encourages houseboat owners to share their experiences, publicizes events of interest, and announces the regattas Sumerset sponsors every year. The regattas draw both owners and prospective customers like the Wollabers, who placed their boat order at a regatta. For people who are interested but can't attend, Sumerset posts updates of the activities and digital snapshots. Sumerset's regattas, which would be far less successful without the Web site's support, represent event marketing par excellence and inspire advertising's most effective technique, word of mouth. The site is such an efficient sales tool that Sumerset no longer needs brokers, who used to sell about a third of the boats the company makes each year. That means the money previously spent on commissions now falls directly to the bottom line.

Sumerset's imaginative use of its Web site is a powerful illustration of the advantages a System TouchPoint has over unpredictable Human TouchPoints. Even the success or failure of a Product TouchPoint can hinge on arbitrary decisions over which your business has no control, such as shelf placement or the selling environment. As a rule, System TouchPoints are less arbitrary. The Sumerset Web site, in particular, exemplifies the TouchPoint ideal because it reliably gives the boat builder's customers experiences and services they can count on. A well-designed and thoroughly tested System TouchPoint puts you in control of your interactions with your customers, and meets my two essential requirements of consistency and scalability.

As a marketing tool Sumerset's Web site could not be more successful. Despite the site's success, however, designer Cecil Helton told *Inc.* that, in the long run, "this is still a niche market. There's only so far it will ever grow." But in my view he is being unnecessarily pessimistic. As the baby boomers retire in ever greater numbers during this decade and the next, houseboats may well follow the trail blazed by recreational vehicles in the 1990s, setting a new lifestyle trend. Moreover, because its System TouchPoint is inherently scalable and independent of location, I don't see why Sumerset shouldn't think about national or global markets.

Sumerset's story and its flourishing Web site offer valuable lessons about optimizing System TouchPoints. Here are three of them:

1. Be flexible, and when serendipity comes knocking, take every advantage. Neckel and Helton creatively devised a simple way to display all the boats being built without infringing on customer privacy, thereby encouraging potential customers to adapt design elements that they might not have thought of otherwise. In addition, when Sumerset's System TouchPoint let the customers view its manufacturing process up close, the company happily used them as unpaid quality-control managers.

2. Humanize your System TouchPoints to avoid putting off people who might lament and resent the loss of human contact to technological replacements. Whereas Sumerset customers used to make frequent visits to check on the progress of their boats, the customized Web site, with its daily pictorial updates, actually got customers even more involved in the details of their boats' construction. What is more, the money Sumerset saved on entertainment entailed no offsetting costs in poor customer relations—just the opposite, it enhanced them. By giving customers an easy way to interact with and control the System TouchPoint it can be even more valuable, as in the case of the Sumerset customer who asked for specific pictures to be posted and immediately had her wishes granted. Technology need not eliminate the human touch altogether, but customers will appreciate the advantages of well-designed System TouchPoints.

3. Look for ways to expand and leverage your System Touch-Points. Sumerset's addition of a used-boat clearinghouse was a natural extension of its brand promise because it draws new buyers who might wish to get their feet wet, so to speak, with a less expensive used houseboat, and it also adds a new and helpful service for current customers wishing to trade up. The regattas are also a powerful tool that simultaneously strengthen customers' ties to the company and to each other, while also attracting new customers, widening the potential market for used boats, and allowing Sumerset to bypass commissioned brokers.

Chico's Systematically Entices and Rewards

Step into a Chico's store and you step into an atmosphere that caters to the affluent American woman (those with an income of one hundred thousand dollars or more) age thirty-five and older. Warm woods, slick metals, and recessed lighting create a backdrop for sophisticated, comfortably designed casual wear in soft, lush,

intensely colored fabrics that are presented with matching accessories. Chico's offers a stylish, easy-to-manage wardrobe for the
woman who wants to look well turned out, perhaps with just a
touch of flamboyance.

Since its founding in 1983, Chico's has evolved into a virtual
money machine. Its operating margin of nearly 21 percent and net
profit margin of 13 percent led the industry in 2003. The company,
which also boasts no long-term debt, operates 445 stores in 46
states under the Chico's name.

Contributing to Chico's continuing success is its effective use of
several System TouchPoints, such as its Passport Club frequent-
buyer program. This TouchPoint rewards shoppers in proportion
to how much they spend in the stores. The Passport Club works because it reinforces the brand promise: We will make it easy and affordable for you to assemble a stylish and comfortable wardrobe.

As soon as a customer spends five hundred dollars (no matter
how long it takes) she becomes a lifelong Passport member. At that
point all her future purchases are discounted by 5 percent. She is
also entitled to free shipping, members-only special sales events,
discount coupons, and advance notice of all sales. Repeat customers who haven't yet reached the five-hundred-dollar threshold
are preliminary Passport members with fewer benefits. Full Passport members account for some 70 percent of Chico's overall sales,
testifying to the critical role this System TouchPoint plays in supporting and enhancing the brand promise.

What is more, Chico's has crafted a series of other System
TouchPoints to support the Passport Club. For instance, Chico's
communicates with its four million Passport members via a glossy,
high-quality catalog it publishes monthly, which includes discount
coupons in various amounts. The catalog generates so much traffic
that 30 to 40 percent of Chico's monthly sales are to shoppers bearing coupons. Incidentally, these shoppers usually spend twice as
much as customers without coupons.

Chico's has also created a database of more than 4.4 million customers. Using data-mining and other software it developed, the chain constantly sends out personalized mailings to lure customers back to its stores. The mailings, which are organized according to age, household income, and individual spending patterns, include catalogs, coupons, even one-hundred-dollar certificates for local restaurants.

Because technology is a vital piece of the infrastructure that fulfills Chico's brand promise to its huge and loyal customer base, the chain has wisely increased its IT investment over the past few years. It spent twenty million dollars on new point-of-sale and back-office systems that were completed in 2001 and 2003, respectively, and another fifteen million dollars went into a state-of-the-art distribution center that can serve twelve hundred stores. Upgraded software systems have enabled the integration of all the company's processes, from product sourcing to warehouse management.

And finally, in what I consider to be a truly creative stroke, Chico's has designed the stores themselves to be a System Touch-Point. As you will recall from my discussion in the previous chapter, a critical element of Chico's Product TouchPoint is its emphasis on wardrobing, including the array of moderately priced accessories and lesser clothing items like T-shirts that can turn a collection of ensemble pieces into a diverse wardrobe. The Chico's stores offer a varied collection of such items. One of the ways Chico's promotes this feature of its Product TouchPoint is through mirrorless dressing rooms. With no mirror to show her how the garment looks a woman must go back out into the store, where she is met by a chorus of helpful salespeople—Human TouchPoints—ready to guide her toward accessories that will complete the outfit. It's a sociable, helpful arrangement that transports a woman back to her teenage years, when girlfriends invariably accompanied one another on shopping trips to suggest styles and accessories, and gives the shopper an honest opinion about how she looks in a chosen piece of clothing. Chico's has made a beautiful marriage of Product, System, and Human TouchPoints that admirably fulfills its brand promise.

Among the many lessons to be found in the Chico's experience are three that will help you to make the most of your System TouchPoints:

1. **Use TouchPoints to reward your customers while at the same time supporting and reinforcing your brand promise.** Chico's Passport Club is both simple and brilliant: It not only gives the chain's customers an incentive—saving money—to increase their purchases, but also helps them to accumulate the stylish, comfortable, and affordable wardrobe that is at the heart of the brand promise. In addition, the glossy catalog that Passport members receive draws customers into the stores and serves as the conduit for those all-important discount coupons.

2. **Make full use of technology to integrate all your processes and enhance your existing System TouchPoints.** The left hand has to know what the right hand is doing. To that end, Chico's has made a substantial investment by installing new point-of-sale and back-office systems and building a state-of-the-art distribution center. By the same token, don't reject technology simply because it isn't leading edge. Sure, Chico's uses high-tech data-mining and other software in creating and targeting its personalized mailings, but the mailings themselves largely consist of catalogs and coupons, technology that harks back to the nineteenth century. Pictures never go out of style, nor do freebies in the form of gift certificates and coupons; they still bring in the shoppers. But Chico's expands the advantage this System TouchPoint offers by using software that allows it to aim its mailings at appropriate-aged women who have the income level and spending habits it seeks.

3. **Don't overlook a potential TouchPoint because of its commonplace characteristics.** Nearly every clothing retailer operates out of a store space with dressing rooms. So ubiquitous are dressing rooms and so standard are their features that it might be easy to overlook them as an opportunity to redesign a System TouchPoint into one that helps you deliver on your brand promise. Not one to miss a chance to excel, Chico's has turned its stores into sociable, customer-friendly places that help fulfill its promise to provide stylish and comfortable wardrobes to its target audience. By leaving mirrors out of its dressing rooms it virtually insists that the women who shop at Chico's interact with one another and with the sales representatives in ways that guarantee a pleasing shopping experience.

Polaroid Grasps at a Saving TouchPoint

Time was when the Polaroid corporation was a secure member of the Nifty Fifty, that 1970s' list of surefire winners that belonged in every stock investor's portfolio. But Polaroid got beaten at its own game: Its brand promise of instant pictures/instant memories was overtaken by the new technology of digital photography, which undermined a business model designed to make money not on the cameras but on the film. For a time Polaroid attempted to compete by going after entry-level users of digital cameras instead of technologically sophisticated ones, but the business proved unprofitable. A load of debt, taken on to avoid a hostile takeover in the 1980s, helped force the company into bankruptcy in 2001, and it exited the digital business. (Polaroid-brand digital cameras are still in the marketplace via a licensing agreement.)

Now, under the wing of its new majority owner, the venture-capital subsidiary of Bank One, Polaroid is fighting back. Success is far from assured, but Polaroid's gambit is intriguing: It's testing a concept that bypasses the costly mainstream of digital photography and could put it back into the competition with a System Touch-Point—speedy new self-service kiosks at which owners of digital cameras can print out their photos cheaply and conveniently. Although most of these kiosks are currently in camera stores, there's no reason they couldn't become as ubiquitous as ATMs.

Kiosks like those Polaroid is testing fill an obvious need in digital photography, which requires no film to be developed and no special training to print out an image. With self-service a photographer can shoot as many frames as he likes and select only the photos he wants to keep. The kiosk business is in its infancy, but competition is already hot. Kodak leads, with twenty-two thousand of its Picture-Maker kiosks already installed. Sony has a deal to put eight hundred of its PictureStations in Kinko's outlets. At this writing, Polaroid is just getting started and has fewer than a dozen kiosks in Boston-area camera shops and an unnamed national retail chain that is about to start test marketing. But Polaroid is betting on the ease, convenience, affordability, and sheer speed of its "2-Second Digital Prints" to reawaken its brand promise: instant gratification.

A user brings her digital camera's memory card to the Polaroid kiosk and uses a touch-screen tutorial to display thumbnail-sized images of the photos it contains. She can print any or all of them. Ten seconds after the print button is pushed, four-by-six-inch prints on glossy Polaroid paper begin dropping from the slot, one every two seconds. All told, 24 digital images can be developed in less than two minutes. The price of 79 cents a print drops to only 39 cents for 20 or more images. Reinforcing the promise of convenience, the kiosks have a slot for swiping a credit card for payment.

Analysts say rival kiosks aren't nearly as fast, and the quality of Polaroid's images, at the very least, matches the field. Its thermal printing technology, called Opal, uses frozen ink on one sheet that liquefies and transfers to another sheet when heated. Bob Barton, Polaroid's director of marketing for the project, told the *Boston Herald* that the photos "look and feel like 35-millimeter prints."

On the face of it Polaroid seems to have a lot of ground to win back. But in a market that is still developing, analysts think Kodak's head start may not be decisive—and Polaroid's brand promise of instant gratification might well regain its old luster.

Win or lose, Polaroid's campaign points up two lessons for optimizing System TouchPoints:

1. Try to leapfrog the pack when you're running behind; get into a new aspect of the business. It would have been much more difficult and expensive for Polaroid to try to catch up to its rivals in the mainstream of digital photography. Instead, it decided to make its stand in photo printing via kiosks.
2. Solidly ground your System TouchPoints in your brand promise and work to reinforce the promise in the customers' minds. The Polaroid brand still evokes the notion of speedy images for photographers, predisposing them to try the new kiosks, which in fact deliver handsomely on the promise.

Progressive Goes the Extra Mile

If "other businesses go the extra mile," asked Progressive's Peter Lewis in a *Fast Company* article, "why not an auto-insurance company?" The chief executive was sincere, but his question was tinged with irony. The insurance business, as Lewis knew full well, is notorious for ever rising premiums and tortoiselike service. His question was the prelude to a total overhaul at Progressive, the Ohio–based insurance holding company whose major line of business is auto insurance. Lewis wanted to do something about the weeks-, if not months-long wait that customers endure to get claims resolved. Because adjusters are expected to process a large number of claims simultaneously, they are inevitably buried in paper and are always working on a backlog.

In 1989, Lewis set out to change the situation by issuing the memo that inaugurated "Immediate Response® claims service," a System TouchPoint designed to resolve claims in hours or days, not weeks. Pushing his idea through despite protests from colleagues, Lewis transformed Progressive from an also-ran into a leader in its industry. In fact, with more than twelve million customers, Progressive is the third-largest auto insurer in the country, based on premiums written.

Immediate Response means that Progressive springs into action 24/7 to give its customers caring, personal service and support immediately after it's notified of an accident or other loss. The process also empowers claims adjusters to settle a claim on the spot, without having to wait for manager approval.

Converting claims processing into a twenty-four-hour operation inspired Progressive's leaders to rethink nearly every aspect of the organization. Lewis created new jobs and assembled teams to expedite each phase of resolving a claim. Today, claims offices around the country radio inquiries and assignments to adjusters, who drive to wherever the customer needs them—even to the scene of an accident—in specially marked SUVs equipped with laptop computers, printers, digital cameras, and cell phones. Few people actually call the company from an accident scene, but Progressive mandates that all vehicles be inspected within nine hours of an accident report.

Progressive's Immediate Response program is an outstanding System TouchPoint for customers because it supports the company's differentiating brand promise: To make insurance easy and understandable, with real service as fast as you need it. Now Progressive's customers feel cared for and sales have soared. The success of Progressive's initiative is also reflected in its financial performance: For 2003, the company reported that net income soared 88 percent to $1.26 billion, or $5.69 a share, on revenues of $11.89 billion, a 28 percent rise from the year-earlier level.

Progressive's initial market niche, high-risk auto insurance, now makes up only about 25 percent of its business, with standard-risk and preferred-coverage policies accounting for the balance. Progressive insures a wide range of personal vehicles, ranging from motorcycles to the two-wheeled Segway, as well as commercial auto and truck policies for small businesses—all of it sold through call centers, on its Web site, and via thirty thousand independent insurance agencies.

Early on, the company was dismayed to discover that some customers were waiting days to report accidents. Delays in the adjustment process can increase the likelihood that a vehicle will be repaired before a claims adjuster can examine it, and may also help those who choose to invent injuries—not to mention the body shops that pad their bills. To reemphasize the company's commitment to making auto insurance easy and understandable Progressive developed its claims card, which resembles a credit card, carries the company's toll-free claims number, has a space for the policy number, and easily breaks in half so that one piece can be given to the other party involved in an accident. Introduction of the claims card has reduced the time in which customers report incidents to hours instead of days.

Progressive's newest System TouchPoint (another first in the industry) introduces true end-to-end service and is extremely convenient for customers whose vehicles are still mobile after an accident: They can drive directly to a claims center, leave their damaged cars, pick up rentals, and know that their cars will be repaired by a Progressive-approved body shop and that the repairs will be inspected and guaranteed by Progressive. Twenty of these centers are already operating.

One of Progressive's main System TouchPoints is its Web site, www.progressive.com. Launched in 1995, the site now draws more than one million visitors every month. Potential customers search the Progressive site more than any other competing site because they can quickly and easily compare Progressive's premiums to those charged by other large insurers. After typing in data about his car a potential customer can get a firm quote on a policy, and by entering his zip code he can get a list of nearby agents who will write the policy. Progressive.com offers easily understood language and strives, said Toby Alfred, the Direct Experience manager, in *PR Newswire*, to "remove the mystery from auto insurance."

In 1996, independent agents, who write about 70 percent of Progressive's policies, got their own dedicated site, www.ForAgentsOnly.com. This System TouchPoint enables agents to access information, make changes to current policies, quote new business, submit applications to the company, and accept payments online.

Progressive followed up in 1998 with www.personal.progressive.com, a System TouchPoint that lets registered customers go online and service their own accounts. The site is most commonly used for "what-ifs," the company says: What will happen to my premium if I trade in the Honda Civic for a Chevy Blazer? What will be the decrease in my collision premium if I raise the deductible to five hundred or a thousand dollars?

Besides providing access to policy information, the site gives policyholders the ability to make payments online and even to change policy details. For instance, a policyholder can change an address, or add a new driver when a son or daughter gets a license, or raise a deductible amount or lower liability limits to reduce the premium. Some agents bemoan this kind of self-service, because it reduces the agent's contact with clients and cuts his or her chances of providing additional service. But the company makes a daily ritual of giving agents a heads-up as soon as a customer makes a change, thus giving them a chance to immediately follow up.

The Gomez Scorecard, which uses a stringent methodology to measure e-commerce offerings and which emphasizes a Web site's educational, purchasing, and service capabilities, has consistently ranked Progressive.com at the top of eighteen analogous sites. Progressive aims to expand this TouchPoint by working on refinements such as electronic billing, online delivery of policy documents, and authentication of e-signatures, among others.

Progressive's set of System TouchPoints provides at least four valuable lessons to companies seeking to make the most of their own TouchPoints:

1. Beat competitors that consistently fail to satisfy customers' basic expectations by designing System TouchPoints that enhance and support your unique brand promise. You will dominate the competitive arena until your rivals can match your moves. Progressive's decision to cut the interminable wait and make claims service quickly available in person 24/7 was the key to its becoming a leader in auto insurance.

2. Be prepared to change all associated processes substantially when you establish an unusually innovative System TouchPoint. Progressive had to revolutionize its internal processes to support its beefed-up level of service, while also changing the way its adjusters worked and adding a fleet of specially equipped vehicles to facilitate on-the-spot resolutions. But the resultant Immediate Response System TouchPoint has been hugely popular with customers and has brilliantly fulfilled Progressive's rejuvenated brand promise.

3. One major new System TouchPoint can open the way for more. After Progressive began its Immediate Response system, it discovered troubling delays in claims reporting. To combat this problem it came up with its claims card, which carries information that facilitates prompt reporting of accidents. Another new TouchPoint that grew out of the Immediate Response system lets customers whose vehicles are still operable drive directly to a claims center after an accident. They pick up rental cars and leave the details of the repairs to Progressive.

   In similar fashion the set of System TouchPoints associated with Progressive's Web site has expanded in several directions since the site was launched in 1995. Initially, the site made it possible for potential customers to compare rates all across the industry. Next, they were able to purchase a policy online in real time, and, later, customers were given the ability to self-service their policies. Meanwhile, Progressive reached out to another of its constituencies, the thirty thousand independent agents who write 70 percent of its business. A separate Web site was created for them, and this System TouchPoint, in turn, has led to more changes in Progressive's processes and has streamlined the writing and processing of policies. To use a timeworn cliché, one good thing can lead to another when it comes to System TouchPoints.

4. Handle disruptive changes with care. When new System Touch-Points threaten to upset existing procedures, let them—but be sensitive to those most affected by the changes. Agents who feared that Progressive's self-service feature would curtail their relationships with clients were nervous, and rightly so. But by making sure that agents were notified promptly of all such changes the agents were able to stay in the loop and could take action to gain additional leverage from their contacts with customers.

Starbucks Pours Its Heart into Innovation

By now, the dimensions of Starbucks's success in developing and fulfilling a differentiating brand promise are well known. The Seattle-based purveyor of specialty coffees counts more than seventy-five hundred stores around the globe and opens between three and four new ones every day, while ringing up double-digit increases in sales and net income year after year. Furthermore, as its thirty million weekly patrons know, the company leverages its success relentlessly by offering a constant stream of new coffees, snacks, coffee-making equipment, and new distribution points for sampling its wares. Its ceaseless innovation is reflected in the way its System TouchPoints work to deliver on its promise to bring high-quality coffees to its customers.

Late in 2001, the corporation introduced the Starbucks Card, a stored-value card that removes the need for a coffee-craving customer to fumble with their wallet or purse at the crucial moment of delivery. Instead of paying cash for your java at each visit, you load up the card in advance; the barista then simply deducts your current charge from the card's available total—a transaction that is completed in a matter of seconds. Even Starbucks's executives were surprised by the card's popularity. In the first quarter, customers bought 2.3 million of the plastic TouchPoints, worth about $32 million, and the pace has only increased since then. The idea of using the cards as Christmas stocking-stuffers boosted sales enormously. Although most of the holiday-card holders threw them away after spending their gift deposits, many reloaded and continued to use the cards.

A year later, Starbucks invited customers to use its Web site for their card-related transactions. They could register their cards online, replace lost cards, add money to their existing cards, and view their card transaction histories. Within months, many cardholders were conducting business online.

Starbucks upgraded the card program late in 2003. Partnering with Visa and Bank One, it issued the Starbucks Card Duetto Visa, which functions as a full-service Visa credit card as well as a prepaid Starbucks Card. The bonus for Starbucks and its customers: 1 percent of the amount charged on the Visa is automatically loaded back onto the Starbucks Card account for use at the stores. In contrast to the airlines' frequent-flyer programs, which can take months or years to pay off, the Duetto arrangement offers quick results. Starbucks sweetens the cup further by contributing five dollars to its nonprofit foundation the first time the related Visa account is used; the foundation is committed to increasing literacy, promoting awareness of diversity issues, and supporting environmental programs.

Starbucks's experience offers you three lessons in how to optimize your System TouchPoints:

1. Keep experimenting. You never know for sure which System TouchPoint will click with customers. The Starbucks Card's prepaid convenience seemed a modest innovation; even company executives were surprised by how many customers found it appealing. And as the card's increasing popularity shows, this is an innovation with legs.
2. Don't underestimate the power of the Web. Especially for trendy young customers like those who frequent Starbucks stores, the appeal of online services, information, and payments is enormous. Within months of devising this System TouchPoint many of the chain's customers were using it.
3. Tune up your TouchPoints with partners. Look for partnerships that can help you overdeliver on your brand promise. Visa and Bank One were so glad to sign up Starbucks customers for their credit card that they were willing to give back a full percentage point of the added volume to be used for prepaid Starbucks products. This System TouchPoint provides an instantly gratifying bonus for the customers—and additional guaranteed revenue for Starbucks.

What's Next

Sumerset, Chico's, Polaroid, Progressive, and Starbucks—these case studies underscore my point that System TouchPoints are among the best ways to support and reinforce your company's differentiating brand promise. They strengthen both Product and Human TouchPoints, but without the inherent unpredictability injected by the human factor. Wherever you can effectively substitute System TouchPoints for in-person service you will enjoy substantial advantages.

But that doesn't mean you can totally eliminate Human TouchPoints. In some businesses human contact is critical, and in nearly every line of business, Human TouchPoints, when used in the right places, can be remarkably effective. The next chapter explains why.

CHAPTER 7

Optimize Your Human TouchPoints

THREE BALD PERFORMERS, whose heads and hands are covered in blue greasepaint, cavort upon the stage through reams of crepe paper. They splash paint, drum on homemade instruments, cut Twinkies with a jigsaw, but like Charlie Chaplin or Buster Keaton before movies had sound, the Blue Men are characters without voices. Using physical stunts, visual gags, and interaction with the audience (volunteers may find their heads encased in Jell-O) the performers make fun of abstract art, information overload, and the fallibility of technology. They speak not a word because their goal is to move beyond words to get their viewers to *feel*. The audience is amused, amazed, and eager to come back for more. They have just witnessed the critically acclaimed Blue Man Group making good on its brand promise to provide unique, thought-provoking, and enormously enjoyable entertainment.

Like any actors, the members of Blue Man Group (BMG) are responsible for a Human TouchPoint the moment their much-ballyhooed brand promise is presented to customers. The means by which they accomplish their task has drawn raves and filled theaters wherever BMG performs—including long-running shows in Boston, Chicago, Las Vegas, and New York, as well as in cities visited by a national touring troupe. The performances, along with Blue Man music CDs and merchandising programs for items like sweatshirts and holiday cards, bring in an estimated $69 million a year.

What piqued my interest in the group is the skillful way in which the original trio developed its brand by improving and enlarging upon its Human TouchPoints.

It began, *Fortune* reports, in 1988 when Chris Wink, Matt Goldman, and Phil Stanton, who were all in their midtwenties, staged a "funeral for the '80s" in Manhattan's Central Park. They donned bald wigs, painted themselves blue, and burned a collection of 1980s' icons that they despised, including yuppie characters and Rambo dolls. So well received was that first production that the group put together a stage show that they performed to packed houses at an off-Broadway theater. The three friends romped through the same routine for twelve hundred performances. Then Stanton cut his hand, and they were forced to bring in an understudy who had never rehearsed the show. To the partners' surprise, he did just fine. New possibilities opened up. The painted anonymity of the Blue Men meant that substitute actors could be hired and the show could be performed in multiple venues. In other words, because their Human TouchPoints were interchangeable their brand was inherently scalable.

In 1995, BMG opened a second production in Boston, but it immediately ran into problems. When Goldman, Stanton, and Wink were not on stage the production lost its focus. With no written script or formal musical score the players were free to improvise, interpreting the performance as they saw fit—but not for long: The three partners wrote out a detailed set of ideas and moves that all Blue Men have followed since. What had been their own intuitive, nonverbal understanding was codified into an operating manual for the brand's Human TouchPoints. The BMG guiding lights made the implicit explicit.

Reproducing the TouchPoints required more than just a manual, however. The cast had to conform to certain standards, so a hiring policy was developed. As long as they are of similar height and build and have acrobatic ability, the actors can be of any nationality or ethnic group, male or female; so far, one woman has made the grade to become a Blue Man. But the key requirement, according to the group's originators, is an in-depth understanding of the spirit and character of BMG. All Blue Men must appreciate the context.

The group's initial off-Broadway success brought a barrage of offers for product endorsements, ad campaigns, and film productions. But Goldman, Stanton, and Wink refused them all. Intent on making Blue Man their careers, they wanted to develop their brand gradually to ensure longevity. They knew that their unique, out-of-the-mainstream quality contributed to their appeal, and could be ruined by too much exposure. So, except for appearing on a few late-night television programs, the trio relied solely on word-of-mouth advertising the first year.

Eventually, the Intel corporation designed an endorsement offer the partners couldn't refuse. They were given artistic control over a series of ads showing the Blue Men interacting with the Intel logo. The ads spread their name to a national audience, paving the way for their expansion.

The founders have made subtle changes in their formula. They have bought advertising to promote shows, and sometimes they use a small band to back up the trio's own music. As they have pursued a larger audience they have kept their focus, stuck to the script, and made sure the core vision of their original brand promise is not compromised.

Getting in Touch with Your Human TouchPoint

A group of performers is not a steel mill or a grocery chain, but the TouchPoint Branding principles are still the same: Businesses succeed by leveraging their Human TouchPoint, which occurs the moment a member of your sales, service, or technical staff interacts in person or over the phone with a customer. The degree to which that interaction fulfills your brand promise depends on how the customer feels about dealing with your employee. And therein lies a problem: The unpredictability of human emotions has entered the equation, making the Human TouchPoint less reliable than the Product and System TouchPoints. Your product will likely live up to your design, manufacturing, and delivery standards, which are largely within your control. You can also be relatively confident that the technology you use for dealing with customers will operate consistently and is scalable. Control and consistency can never be guaranteed, however, when it comes to the Human TouchPoint. (Later in this chapter I will discuss some ways to bring as much certainty as possible to the Human TouchPoint.)

Despite its unpredictability, the Human TouchPoint remains essential to your ongoing mission of overdelivering on your brand promise, and humans used in the right ways can bring enormous value to your brand. Numerous occasions arise in which a customer needs a personal touch; the electronic variety just won't do. A woman walks into your store and finds a coat she likes, but she has concerns: Is it the right color for her? Will it work in a business setting? Is it appropriate for her age? Another customer explains that he paid for an extended warranty when he bought your company's computer two years ago, but he didn't send in the registration card and now he's lost the warranty number. A long-term corporate customer is shocked that your company wants to increase her fee; she's talking about taking her business elsewhere.

When the situation is complicated or ambiguous, when patience, flexibility, and initiative are required to hold on to a customer or win a new one, you have to rely on your frontline people to save the day. That's when the Human TouchPoint is your best solution, essential, really, for overdelivering on your brand promise. Only your employees can empathize, improvise, or override the rules. They alone can relate to customers as fellow human beings.

In some businesses the Human TouchPoint reigns supreme. People staying at a Ritz-Carlton hotel, for instance, want more than a comfortable bed and a hot shower. They expect the luxury hotel experience, and that means extraordinary human service with a winning smile. The hotel's fine linens, handcrafted furniture, and French-milled soaps are part of the luxury experience, but not the centerpiece. Each of Ritz-Carlton's fifty-seven hotels, resorts, spas, golf clubs, and other plush facilities is a study in personal service— a global Human TouchPoint.

The Ritz Paris, for example, has a staff of more than 500 to serve only 106 rooms, 56 suites, and 11 apartments. At a Ritz-Carlton hotel, where a single martini may set you back $17, the bellmen are authorized to spend as much as $2,000 to help you solve a problem. If you ask for directions to a location inside the hotel, you won't get an answer; instead, you'll get an escort. All requests are met with the response, "It would be my pleasure, sir (or madam)." Service like this doesn't come cheap, but to paraphrase J. P. Morgan's famous observation about yachting, the Ritz clientele doesn't have to ask what it costs; they can afford it.

Like the founding members of the Blue Man Group, who understood the unpredictability of human interactions and did all they could to counter it by developing a script and designing hiring policies that support it, winning companies pay close attention to the quality of their Human TouchPoint. Harley-Davidson's turnaround in the 1980s, when the company was on the brink of bankruptcy, depended not only on improving the product, but customer relations as well. The legendary motorcycle manufacturer formed the Harley Owners Group, or H.O.G., so that buyers of its bikes would feel they belonged to a community. The group's success helped to save the company. But by the late 1990s, Harley's leaders recognized that H.O.G.'s tough, clannish reputation was costing it market share by frightening away potential new customers, particularly novice motorcyclists who were also nervous about the size and weight of the machines.

Harley responded by developing an instruction class for neophytes called the Rider's Edge. Not the typical three-hour event, Rider's Edge is a two-and-a-half-day affair during which participants spend almost sixteen hours driving on an asphalt range in the saddle of a Buell, a lighter, less expensive bike also made by Harley. Along the way they pass all the written and road tests demanded for certification by the Motorcycle Safety Foundation (MSF)—and if they fail, Harley won't sell them a machine.

The goal, said Lara Lee, director of Rider's Edge, is to help newcomers feel like insiders. And to keep experienced cyclists from feeling deserted, Harley has developed a special self-study video seminar on riding in groups and also offers, in conjunction with the MSF, a course to help advanced riders cope with potentially dangerous situations. The Rider's Edge thus adds a new dimension to Harley's Human TouchPoint that brings customers ever closer to the company while at the same time enriching its brand promise.

Beware Overreliance on Human TouchPoints

It's true that Human TouchPoints are critical in virtually every business, but they do have their limits. Many organizations rely on their frontline people more than they should, which implies that other TouchPoints, particularly the System TouchPoint, are not being optimized.

Look around your business. How much of what your people do must be done by humans? In many companies people regularly handle functions that could be delivered more simply, effectively, less expensively, and consistently in other ways. Doing so would free up your people to deliver far higher value to customers. Worse yet, you are consigning your company's fate to the vagaries of unpredictable human relationships.

The folly of trusting your company's fate to "heroes" is nowhere better exemplified than in the tale of Nordstrom. The Seattle-based upscale clothing chain has been a legendary service provider almost since the day in 1901 when John W. Nordstrom first started selling shoes. Nordies, as employees call themselves, thought nothing of custom-suiting a frantic business traveler after lunch in time for dinner, or personally delivering shoes to a customer one hundred miles away because overnight mail service would be too slow.

This is what I call heroics-based customer service, and it was appropriate and appreciated when Nordstrom served a small, elite clientele willing to pay for the heroics. But it won't work for big companies in mass markets with thousands of employees. Just think about it: How strong is a business model predicated on delivering heroic service? And where do you find all those people willing to do the heroics on their personal time? Regression to the mean ensures that even if you start out with all heroes, scaling will result in more and more nonheroes being hired, weakening the fulfillment of your brand promise.

Nordstrom is a case in point. As it expanded rapidly in recent years—it now has 148 stores in 27 states, 92 of which are full-line stores—it tried in vain to maintain its heroic customer service, ignoring the fact that it was increasingly unable to keep its brand promise. As a result, overall customer service declined. Labor shortages made good (read: heroic) salespeople hard to find. Staffers sued the chain for unpaid overtime and alleged harassment as managers pushed to meet hourly sales quotas; Nordstrom settled the suit for $22 million. Meantime, the chain's once bouncy image turned stodgy. Intent on boosting its share price to finance expansion, Nordstrom had neglected its emotional ties to younger customers, who jumped ship. Earnings plunged 50 percent in fiscal 2001.

Nordstrom plans to add still more stores, but realizes that revitalized, consistent customer service aimed at both older and younger generations is critical, if not the ticket for its survival. What is clearly required is a full-scale rebirth of consistently good service and selection for all of the company's customers. At this writing, Nordstrom's rejuvenated brand promise, supported by a more realistic Human TouchPoint, is working its magic: In the three months ended May 1, 2004, both same-store and overall sales were strong, rising 13.2 percent and 16.6 percent, respectively, while earnings jumped an astonishing 153 percent from the year-earlier level.

Recognizing the pros and cons of Human TouchPoints you must assess where you stand. Have you assigned sufficient resources to support your salespeople and service representatives? Does your company's culture inspire them to achieve? Are you providing the right kind of environment and incentives? Have you developed the best hiring and training programs in your market?

This chapter will show you how to answer these questions with a resounding "Yes!" The pages ahead contain case histories of companies that, like the Blue Man Group, have designed superb Human TouchPoints to help fulfill their brand promises, and each has lessons to teach. In fact, let's begin with those men in blue to see what your business can take away from their experiences:

1. Prepare the script. If you want your frontline people to behave in a particular manner—and surely you do—heed Blue Man's example and give them a script to follow. Make it as detailed as you think necessary, but I would err on the side of giving too much rather than too little information. It should spell out what each customer interaction should look like, sound like, and feel like. Sure, you want to leave room for intelligent and intuitive experimentation by your sales and service people at the Human TouchPoint, but you also want them to know when and why they are deviating from the norm—and that assumes they know what the norm is. You must make the implicit explicit. When Chris Wink and his partners worked out their operating manual it was 132 pages long. It was full of insights ("The Blue Men are not aliens") and literary and theatrical references. Your version

is likely to be more prosaic, but the goal is the same: to provide consistency and scalability at the Human TouchPoint.

2. Hire to the script. Any normally capable person can read the manual and follow directions. For your Human TouchPoint to reach its full potential you need to hire and train people who will live the manual. Blue Man Group looks for people who understand and embody the essential character of their roles. You should do the same. Don't hire someone who can simply "act" friendly and helpful. The characteristics you seek should be second nature to the people you hire—no acting involved. In other words, if you want your sales representatives to maintain a smiling, upbeat presence, you better be certain that those you hire have naturally pleasant, optimistic personalities. Qualities like that cannot be faked over the long haul. In fact, skillful hiring is the best and easiest way to improve every aspect of your company—from its culture to its everyday performance to its ability to fulfill your brand promise.

3. Train to the script. Newcomers to the ranks of your frontline staff must be trained to master the operating manual just as Blue Man newcomers are trained in the actions and ideas that define a Blue Man performance. Your new salespeople should also be indoctrinated in the spirit that informs the script and the brand promise—in other words, they must understand the context, not just the text.

So far, we've concentrated on newcomers, but don't forget about your veterans. All too often companies ignore the very real need to retrain experienced frontline staffers. Not so at winning companies. They invest in retraining to keep everyone on the front line up-to-date and in sync with rejuvenated brand promises. It should come as no surprise that the longer an employee stays in a job, the more bad habits and attitudes he or she is likely to pick up. It is all too easy to get stuck doing something—like greeting potential customers, for example—in a way that may have worked better a few years ago, when most of your customers were younger or perhaps less knowledgeable than they are today. A service representative may rely on a certain sequence in making a customer call that no longer concurs with recent changes in your script.

Admittedly, you may not want to invest as much time or money as, say, the Container Store, whose veteran full-time employees receive 160 hours of training each year. However, you should program a regular refresher course into the schedules of all frontline people. Regular retraining can help keep your Human Touch-Point from drifting out of line with your brand promise.

4. Market through your script. Follow the Blue Man Group's example: It shied away from spending on conventional promotions and relied instead on word-of-mouth advertising. The money saved is only the first benefit. Traditional advertising, as I mentioned earlier, can't capture the essence of many brands. It can greatly expand public awareness of a brand's existence, of course, but simple recognition doesn't translate directly into sales. The glowing report of a friend or acquaintance who has personally experienced your product's superiority at the Human TouchPoint will convince more new customers to try it, and they too will pass on the approval through word of mouth. What more could you ask for?

The Richard Petty Driving Experience

Strapped into the race car's driver's seat, 630 horses raring to go, you sit watching the flagman up ahead. He finally gives you the "go" sign and you ease up on the clutch while feeding her gas. The car glides along an oval track where some of the greatest names in NASCAR history have made their marks. Gradually, you move up through the gears until you reach fourth, then you floor it. The engine roar is deafening. The forward thrust pushes you back almost through your seat. As your speed climbs, the centrifugal force pushes you hard to the right: 100 . . . 125 . . . 140 m.p.h. You are flying!

That's the ultimate thrill the Richard Petty Driving Experience offers at twenty-five tracks around the country. Petty is a seven-time NASCAR national champion in a sport whose popularity has exploded over the last decade, and his Concord, North Carolina–based company has flourished right along with it. Petty's one hundred thousand paying customers, both drivers and passengers, log over 2.5 million track miles a year. From the moment you climb into your fire suit to the moment you squeeze out of the car and find out your fastest lap speed, every step has been carefully calculated to give you a realistic sense of what it's like to be a NASCAR driver. The vehicle you drive duplicates the real thing in appearance and performance, except for somewhat lower horsepower. Your name is announced over the track's public address system as you prepare to drive. There is no passing—for safety's sake, every driver must follow an instructor's car around the track. But once you demonstrate the ability to control your car and maintain the proper distance from the lead vehicle, you can drive as fast as the instructor and the particular track permit.

Before you're allowed anywhere near a racing car, though, you're put through a lengthy training process. You watch a video in which the King—Petty's track nickname—warns you of the potential hazards ahead. The cars are fast: They can get away from you quickly and spin easily if you're not careful. An instructor drives you around the track in a van, pointing out the cones that alert you when to take your foot off the gas and when to accelerate. After a few more driving tips you are introduced to your car. You learn how to shift and how to operate the fire-extinguisher system. A track employee helps get you into the driver's seat, helmeted, and strapped in. But after he starts the engine you are on your own.

Petty offers all sorts of racing-car thrills. The Rookie Experience, for example, is a three-hour program that gives you eight laps around the track for about four hundred dollars. The King's Experience, a five-hour program with eighteen laps, costs about twice as much. For about $125, you can ride shotgun to a professional driver.

The company has grown tremendously over the fourteen years since it first put the public into racing cars. And it has achieved success by following some of the very same principles explained in this book. Petty has developed a powerful brand promise—to provide safe, reliable, authentic motor sports entertainment—and fulfilled it admirably. (There has not been a single injury among the company's many thousands of customers.) It has built its brand by first identifying thirty-one TouchPoints at which it interacts with customers, and then devising a quality assurance process around each of them. And by investing virtually all of its resources in improving its customers' experience, the company has avoided major outlays for advertising and promotion. It relies instead on word of mouth.

One of the most important of the company's thirty-one customer-centric TouchPoints is its call center, which handles more than 150,000 calls annually. Some years ago new employees at this Human TouchPoint were trained by veterans who sat down with the newcomers and showed them what to do and how to do it. The operators then tried their hand at the process, and supervisors gave them a bit of feedback. The results, however, were very uneven, and the training period sometimes stretched over three or four weeks.

Then Petty began using a computer-based training tool, called Communication Coach, developed by Success Sciences of Tampa, Florida, a company that specializes in bringing certainty to the human element of the customer experience. This technology allows new hires to listen to and study dozens of simulated conversations in which callers receive ideal treatment from employees. The conversations are completely customized to the culture and brand promise of the client company, reflecting its views on what should be said, in what order, and how. For example, the tone of the employee's voice and the speed and volume of delivery are dictated by the client company and the product or service it is offering. Trainees record their own practice sessions responding to callers, and then toggle back and forth between the model and their own versions, noting differences along the way. This comparison feature also enables a trainee's supervisor to provide precisely focused feedback and reinforcement. In addition, the Communication Coach teaches new call-center employees how to navigate through the company's software system and provides information about the company's products, policies, and procedures.

I asked Frank Vari, Petty's executive vice president, to spell out the business benefits of the Communication Coach approach. "In the old days," he said, "you were always like, okay, I think they can do the job. You had your fingers crossed. Now we know for certain that they will do the job, and do it well." And instead of three or four weeks, the computer training takes just two. Vari also noted a positive change in the operators' attitudes. "Far more than in the past, they're trying to understand what individual customers need and trying to find ways to drive the sale." As a result, the company's confirmation rate has risen sharply. Before computer training, "we were able to convert to business about 10 percent to 12 percent of the incoming calls," Vari said. "Now, we're up to 18 percent or 19 percent, and that [level has] held for two years or so."

What Vari calls "up-sell" has been much better, too. "When someone calls for a Rookie Experience, instead of just saying, 'OK, let me get your name and number' and so forth, the operators say, 'Would you also like to buy a ride-along for your guest? Or would you like to upgrade to a King's Experience, which is a higher-valued program?' So that's part of our repertoire now." Vari estimated that the phone center's revenue per call has risen 10 percent or more. "We are so pleased with the results we've gotten from Communication Coach that we are now investigating their Selection Coach product."

Clearly, the company's Human TouchPoint has benefited enormously from its use of a computer-training program. Here are four lessons you can draw from the Petty company's experience:

1. Consistency counts. The Petty operation started with the romantic and dramatic idea of giving racing fans a chance to experience firsthand some of the thrills of being a NASCAR driver. To make sure that happened for every customer every time the company had to build the right kind of cars and design a process that would be safe for customers, instructors, and the cars themselves. It also had to convince tracks around the country to welcome the program. Finally, it had to fashion a Human TouchPoint, supported by technology, that would seamlessly lead customers through the other TouchPoints of the experience, start to finish. Once its method was developed, the company made sure it would be followed to the letter at all its sites. "It's no different from McDonald's," Frank Vari said. "We want to make sure you have the same great experience wherever you go. We want repeat customers, and we get them." The computerized-training program strongly reinforced the consistency of the company's Human TouchPoints.

2. Use the technology fix. Yes, the success of your Human Touch-Points, by definition, depends on the effectiveness of your human resources. But you need to consider all tools available to guide your frontline people to the best customer approach, whether they work in call centers or at a sales counter. Today's technology can be a most effective substitute for traditional training approaches.

Some of my clients are now using BrainX software to dramatically improve retention of product knowledge while reducing learning time. The software was originally developed for busy medical professionals who risked losing their licenses and practices if they failed a recertification exam. BrainX patented software decreased study time by an average of 11 percent, while improving test scores by an average of 80 percent. Because the software can be used to study any information you want to master, I immediately began sharing it with my clients to enhance their employees' product knowledge. (In fact, I'm so excited about the potential of Brainx software, I've provided a copy of it on the CD in the back of this book.)

Computer-based training doesn't produce the friction that often occurs in a teacher-student relationship involving adults, and it can take place when and where the trainee chooses to learn. Enabling a new hire to learn the job pretty much free of interference improves self-confidence and self-respect, which make that person a more effective frontline worker. Though the initial investment may be substantial, as the Petty company discovered, such technological fixes pay for themselves sooner rather than later.

3. Recognize the limits of technology. As potent as computer training can be in preparing frontline employees for their assignments, it can't do the whole job. As the Petty driving school discovered, you and your managers will in the end have to judge whether trainees are meeting your standards of performance. You will have to monitor how trainees are doing with software you select, and provide whatever personal training is necessary.

Technological tools have their place in supporting Human TouchPoints, but they also have their limits. They can be ingenious, cost-effective, and thorough, but no computer program can give the individual attention and reinforcement a frontline employee may need to get the most out of the training. In other words, don't expect technology to totally eliminate the need for human interaction in training, coaching, and leadership. The role of software is to shorten the learning cycle and bring much-needed consistency to the Human TouchPoint.

4. Customize. As a general rule, building an effective TouchPoint of any kind requires you to tailor the process to your company, your brand promise, and the particular customers you're trying to reach. In Vari's view, that was the key to the success of the Communication Coach program at Petty. "We customized the scenarios to handle the situations that we were dealing with, and to handle our unique challenges. That's what made the difference." Customers in every business pose different sorts of questions and problems, and your Human TouchPoints must be form-fitted.

The Container Store—the Best Place to Work

Everyone agrees that engaging human interactions are a basic ingredient of a breakthrough Human TouchPoint. The Container Store is a role model for that kind of service. The Dallas, Texas–based retail chain, which offers some ten thousand storage and organization products, grounds its brand promise in this simple reality: The company hires fewer frontline people than its competitors, trains and coaches them superbly, and pays them from 50 to 100 percent more than the going industry average. That's what I call a win-win situation.

Kip Tindell, the company's cofounder and chief executive, would seem to agree: "A funny thing happens when you take the time to educate your employees, pay them well, and treat them as equals," he told *Workforce* magazine. "You end up with extremely motivated and enthusiastic people." And in the case of the Container Store, you also end up with a thirty-one-store, privately owned empire that stretches across the country and achieves sales growth of at least 20 percent a year.

Walk into a Container Store and you enter a world very different from any other retail environment. Instead of shoes, dresses, or television sets there are shelves, racks, bags, and boxes arranged in rooms—kitchen, closet, office, laundry. Instead of salespeople who ignore you the Container Store is staffed by smiling, friendly folks in blue aprons who are happy to greet you and seem to enjoy their jobs. They also listen carefully, respond intelligently, and suggest ingenious space- and time-saving solutions designed to simplify your life.

Tindell and partner Garrett Boone, the chairman, opened the first Container Store in Dallas in 1978. It wasn't all smooth sailing. They had a computerized inventory system that didn't work and headaches caused by too much growth too fast. The realization that they were also hiring the wrong people led to the development of a set of principles that have guided the company and its employees ever since. Among them:

- Fill the other guy's basket to the brim. Making money then becomes an easy proposition.
- Apply the Golden Rule in all encounters, creating an environment of trust with customers, vendors, and fellow employees.
- Create a sense of excitement in every store.
- Be Gumby. The reference is to the corporation's mascot, the green toy notable for its incredible flexibility, but the message is a familiar one: Make the implicit explicit.
- Train intensely so that your intuitive leaps are based upon research, not guesswork.

All first-year, full-time Container Store employees receive 235 hours of training, compared to the industry average of 7 hours; new part-timers get 150 hours of training. All new employees—including office staff—spend their first week working in a store. As mentioned previously, veteran full-timers get an average of 160 hours of training each year. Very little turnover is what makes such intensive training affordable for the company. At the Container Store the turnover rate for all full-time employees is 8 percent and for part-timers, 20 percent. Contrast that to an industry average of 120 percent.

Intensive, hands-on training is particularly important at the Container Store because of the multitude of products it offers and the "man-in-the-desert," comprehensive-solutions principle it espouses. A man lost in the desert for days may ask rescuers for water, but he also needs food, a chance to call his family, a place to sleep. By the same token, a customer may ask just for something to keep his shirts in, but he may actually need to have his whole closet reorganized. So when approaching a customer's problem employees are encouraged to think big, beyond the boundaries, in order to devise a great solution that not only wows the customer, but as it usually turns out, also sells more products. Container Store frontline people are well prepared to recognize any need and satisfy it.

An emotional response is what Container Store employees are after. What evokes that emotional response is the relationship Container Store sales reps establish at the Human TouchPoint, which in turn is a function of their very positive attitudes toward their jobs and their company. For several years now Container Store has been at or near the top of *Fortune* magazine's list of "100 Best Companies to Work For." A conversation with the company's employees explains why. They talk about wanting to come to work, about enjoying the interaction with customers, about a culture in which "people care about each other."

Sales reps are encouraged to make their own decisions when they work with customers, and if the customer's problem is a complex one, frontline people respond as a team, discussing various ideas and arriving at a unique solution. Having hired the best people, paid them handsomely, trained them thoroughly, and indoctrinated them in the culture, the company expects them to perform at their peak. And they do.

Here are some lessons drawn from the Container Store experience to help you make the most of your Human TouchPoints:

1. Put it on paper. In my view, most companies do not live up to their brand promises. A company's leaders need to determine the essence of their brand, all the things that make it distinctive, and then make sure the promise is thoroughly understood and accepted by their frontline employees. The Container Store, which promises unparalleled service in helping customers find unique storage ideas, achieves this goal in part by having a set of six principles that trainers and managers discuss with newcomers. When your Human TouchPoint truly reflects your brand promise you will realize a new level of sales and profitability.

2. Hire top talent. There's no denying it's expensive, not only because you have to pay high salaries, but also because you have to create an environment that will make employees want to stay around. But as the Container Store's experience shows, you can recoup your investment by decreasing turnover and increasing productivity and sales. The work ethic of the frontline people, combined with their commitment to teamwork, enables the Container Store to upgrade the level of its Human TouchPoint while staffing its outlets with far fewer sales representatives than is typical in its industry.

3. Invest in training. What you spend on top talent will be wasted unless you provide the training and education that will perfect your Human TouchPoints. Your new employees need to know that you want something more than just getting the job done; you want it done magnificently. At the Container Store new hires are taught how the thousands of products can be manipulated to answer individual customers' needs. The training starts by placing newcomers in the stores so they can see firsthand how sales representatives help customers; it continues in group classes and one-on-one tutorials. Even seasoned veterans receive

instruction to bring them up-to-date on the newest products and sales approaches. To demonstrate the long-term effectiveness of its intensive training the Container Store cites this statistic: Over the last two decades the number of dollars spent by each customer has more than doubled, from the low twenties to almost fifty dollars.

4. Focus on values. It is crucial to create an environment of mutual trust. The Container Store incorporates that goal in its principles, at the center of which is the Golden Rule: Trust between leaders and employees allows management to redirect a frontline person's energy without incurring anger. It also allows an employee to experiment with new ideas without fear of punishment if the initiative doesn't pan out. Trust between employees enables productive teamwork without competitive rancor, and putting salespeople on a salary (as opposed to a commission) removes any reason to feel jealous over another's success. Employees are also kept informed about the state of the business and are consulted before key decisions are made. They see that the generous benefits and salaries, as well as the recognition of special achievement, are distributed fairly. Once mutual trust exists your frontline people will be enthusiastic about elevating your company's Human TouchPoint.

5. Leave them alone. Once you have hired, trained, and indoctrinated the very best people you can find they will be better equipped than you or your managers to help customers. Nothing should hinder them from exercising their knowledge, intuition, and initiative. At the Container Store the Human TouchPoint works best when sales and service people are encouraged to think like owners, improving existing approaches and devising new ones on the spot. Garrett Boone tells of a salesman in Maryland who discovered, while checking out a customer, that the closets in the woman's new home were completely disorganized. The salesman closed the register and set

about planning new closets for her. At a store in Chicago, Boone relates in *D* magazine, a customer's car seat got ripped when the just-purchased items were being placed in her car. When the saleswoman heard what happened she immediately took cash from the register and paid the customer for the damage. Top-notch frontline people need the freedom to do their jobs.

Edward Jones—It's All About Relationships

The brokerage firm of Edward Jones is in many ways out of step with today's financial marketplace. Its headquarters are in St. Louis, Missouri, not New York. Its clients are long-term individual investors such as retirees and small-business owners, not multimillionaire ticker-watchers or hard-eyed institutions. And a customer who wants to buy or sell a stock has to call his broker or meet with her in person: Although customers can e-mail their brokers, online trading is simply not available. Edward Jones's representatives don't just execute orders, they build relationships, and the firm refuses to let technology interfere with that. In other words, Jones relies heavily on its Human TouchPoint to deliver on the firm's brand promise.

The people who staff Jones's 9,000 offices in the United States, as well as more than 550 in Canada and nearly 100 in the United Kingdom, are expected to become part of the communities in which they operate, and trusted financial advisers to their clients. Investment representatives are the cornerstone, says John Bachmann, the longtime managing partner of Jones who stepped down at the end of 2003. Because they are the firm's only profit center everything hinges on how well the reps serve the retirees and small-business owners that make up the bulk of Jones's clientele.

By all accounts the Jones reps are remarkably effective. Revenue has doubled since 1997, reaching $2.3 billion in 2003, a year in which the firm earned $142 million. By contrast, members of the

Securities Industry Association experienced a 24 percent decline over 2002 revenues.

A *Darwin* magazine story described the experience of a typical Jones investment representative, Melanie Shuffield, who opened an office in Cameron, Texas, in 1989. She began by joining the Chamber of Commerce, the Rotary Club, and the Methodist Church, and spent her first months walking around town and knocking on doors to introduce herself. Today she has thousands of accounts and handles millions in assets, but Shuffield stays in touch on a personal level, sending out birthday, sympathy, and get-well cards. Those with ten thousand dollars to invest are as welcome as those with ten times that amount. Shuffield knows her clients and their individual circumstances well enough to tailor her advice to their needs—and to argue against their making a wrong move. When they do make a particularly big trade she sends her thanks in the form of a bag of jelly beans.

Jones has perfected its approach to hiring, training, and rewarding its Human TouchPoint representatives. Of the one hundred thousand applicants for investment representative jobs each year the firm hires just 8 percent. Most of the people it does take on are former teachers, accountants, and salespeople—"high achievers with a sense of purpose" in the words of John Bachmann in a *Financial Executive* interview. Only 20 percent have any previous brokerage experience.

The firm invests seventy-five thousand dollars in the training of new representatives; that includes the cost of mentoring them for the Series 7 examination, which potential financial representatives are required to pass. Employees receive an average of 149 hours of training annually.

Successful representatives are well rewarded by Edward Jones. More than five thousand of its employees are limited partners, receiving a share of all profits. It encourages its people to think like owners. For the first year after they pass the Series 7 exam representatives get a two-thousand-dollar-a-month guaranteed base salary plus commissions and bonuses on new accounts they open. After that they work on commission only. The median W-2 earnings of a Jones rep after two years are more than $55,000; after five years, they top $120,000.

Like the Container Store, Edward Jones is at the top rung of *Fortune*'s list of "100 Best Companies to Work For." In part, that reflects its benefits, its continuing education mandate, and its efforts to maintain a connection with its distant outposts. Bachmann provided another explanation to *Financial Executive:* "Our employees love working here because of the alignment between our activities and the needs of our customers." That's also why the firm's Human TouchPoint is so successful.

Even though Jones rules out online trading for its clients because it denies the very relationship upon which the firm is based, the firm has nothing against using the Internet and other System TouchPoints in its own trading and back-office operations. By utilizing the best of both worlds—the efficiency of technology and the connections of its Human TouchPoint—Edward Jones is able to deliver on its promise of a personalized approach to high-quality, long-term investing.

Here are some lessons from the Jones story to help you optimize your Human TouchPoint:

1. Go all out. The more you depend upon any one TouchPoint to fulfill your brand promise, the greater the effort must be to maintain its quality, but Human TouchPoints require special attention. When Edward Jones decided to cast its lot with the individual investor the firm understood that its future would depend upon how effective its investment representatives were at building lasting relationships with their clients. To smooth the way Jones has devoted enormous resources to the preparation and support of these frontline people. Their training is ex-

tensive; their culture is performance-oriented; their rewards are substantial. The result: a wildly successful Human Touch-Point.

2. The magic is in the details. Melanie Shuffield's path is familiar to anyone who has tried to start a service business. Whether you're a lawyer, an accountant, or a sales representative you join clubs and knock on doors to become known and start building relationships. Shuffield's attention to detail—the birthday cards and jelly beans, for example—is worth noting. It's easy to slack off on tending a relationship once it's established, and then, before you know it, the relationship is coming apart at the seams. To sustain a Human TouchPoint you need to make sure your frontline people realize that the magic resides in the details—in the welcoming smile, in remembering to ask about a customer's health and family, in the complete attention you give the customer while talking with her. If you haven't done so already, prepare and distribute a checklist of such details to your frontline managers. Reward those sales and service people who keep the magic alive.

3. Stick to your guns. It takes courage to hold to your vision when everyone else is moving in another direction. That's as true in business as it is in politics or religion. When the rest of the industry seized upon the Internet as a way to satisfy do-it-yourself investors while devoting more resources to larger accounts Edward Jones refused to let technology compromise the representative-client relationship.

4. Revitalize with outsiders. If you want to stand out as unique in your industry, as a company that deviates from the business-as-usual approach, you will have a rough time if your new hires are all industry insiders. It's more than likely that their attitudes, beliefs, and mind-sets are so ingrained as to make it virtually impossible to successfully rejuvenate your Human TouchPoint. Old hands will always have a tendency to revert to the past way

of doing things. Eighty percent of Jones's new hires in any given year come from outside the brokerage industry. All are high achievers, but their experience varies. Many are former teachers, accountants, and salespeople—some of the very same people, in fact, who make up the individual-investor group Jones caters to. So besides gaining the benefit of outside opinions and diverse experiences, Jones also gains representatives who know and understand its target clientele.

Bellagio—Hiring 9,600 People in Twenty-four Weeks

Since Las Vegas is a desert resort jam-packed with hotels, a new one must be very special to make a splash. In 1998, Bellagio established itself as a singular sensation. Aside from being gigantic and elegant, with three thousand rooms furnished in European style, Bellagio boasts a magical botanical garden filled with exotic plants and flowers and a fine art gallery loaded with old masters. Several times a day its choreographed fountains provide a spectacular music-and-light show. What holds it all together, though, is a staff of 9,600 employees, most of whom deliver admirably on the hotel's brand promise to provide the best of everything. How that staff was hired in a mere twenty-four weeks offers some important lessons for any organization seeking to get the best at its Human TouchPoint.

Here's the Bellagio miracle in a nutshell: The hotel screened 84,000 applicants in the first 12 weeks. It interviewed 27,000 finalists in 10 weeks. It processed the winning candidates, almost 10,000 of them, in 11 days. And it was all accomplished by putting together one of the first fully integrated, online job-application and hiring programs. The System TouchPoint was drawn into service to support the Human TouchPoint. Open database architecture made it possible for client-server and browser technologies to do their work, and for the hotel to put together a talented staff using barely a single piece of paper.

There were 633 job classifications, ranging from dealers at the blackjack tables to front-desk clerks and accountants. Applications had to be filled in online at computer terminals in the hotel offices. The project's size and tight deadline meant the application process had to be streamlined. But at the same time it had to be crystal clear, and the prompts easy to follow. The 168 questions on the application were designed to take about forty-eight minutes to complete. During the first phase one hundred computer terminals were busy twelve hours a day, six days a week, nonstop.

Arte Nathan, the former vice president for human resources who oversaw this operation, decided that applicants should be treated like Bellagio guests, with a maximum of courtesy and respect. A candidate who drove into the parking lot was welcomed by a hotel staff person. That staff person addressed each candidate by name and assigned her or him to a terminal that also recognized the name. "I wanted to . . . impress the hell out of them," Nathan told *Fast Company*, "and convert them from casually interested to very interested."

When candidates finished their applications the computer expressed the company's appreciation and directed them to a checkout desk. Bellagio management could simply have sent candidates to the exit, but it wanted to give a human resources representative a chance to observe each candidate's behavior and communication skills. One in five applicants was turned down on the basis of that brief interaction.

Personal interviews were conducted not by HR people, but by managers of the individual job areas specially trained for the task. Each interview was limited to a maximum of thirty minutes. The Web-based database enabled managers to find the candidates who rated highest for, say, front-desk jobs, and to then select three people to interview for each opening. At the interviews the managers asked candidates a set of questions developed by Nathan and his aides that probed attitudes and behavioral patterns. A difficult circumstance might be described, for example, with several possible responses to choose from. The answers were entered into the database, which tallied each candidate's score.

Once a manager settled on a particular candidate, employment and education histories were checked. About 8 percent of the candidates were eliminated by these background checks. Those who made it through and also passed a drug test were invited to a job-offer session.

Generally, companies have three separate paper files on a new hire—a personnel file, an Equal Employment Opportunity Commission file, and a medical file. But Bellagio was able to combine the information into a single electronic file. It even devised paperless personnel and payroll forms, which managers filled out online. All in all, the technology developed for the hiring campaign saved the company $1.9 million. And it provided the hotel with a first-rate staff that has an enviable track record in making the most of its Human TouchPoint.

What lessons can your company take away from the Bellagio example?

1. Marry multiple TouchPoints. The traditional hiring process can be a disaster. The decision to hire or pass is often made arbitrarily on the basis of a hunch or a misheard or misunderstood comment. The Bellagio saga shows how the application of modern technology can strip the interview of some of its uncertainties and help assure that the best person for the job will be chosen.

   Note, though, that in this marriage of System and Human TouchPoints, Bellagio made sure that the human side was not overwhelmed. At every stage the hotel strove to treat job candidates with the same courtesy and respect it wanted them to show its guests. Indeed, Bellagio was practicing a policy that is common among successful companies and their top managements seeking to maximize Human TouchPoints: Lead the way, showing by your own decisions and behavior what you hold to be important. Technology can make a big contribution to the efficiency of your hiring policy, but it can never completely replace the human touch.

2. Dig deep. Bellagio had little time to accomplish a monumental task. Nevertheless, the hotel was determined to find the kind of people who would deal pleasantly and efficiently with its guests. So it went to great lengths to uncover the personal qualities of its job candidates, even though the bulk of the hiring process was handled electronically. In the first screening stage candidates were directed to a staff person who looked over the online application, theoretically to make sure all questions were answered. In fact, the staff person's main responsibility was to observe and report any behavioral characteristics that would be either inappropriate or advantageous for the job sought. Also, in constructing its model personal interview sessions the company used behavioral interviewing techniques, designing questions that would elicit information about candidates' likely conduct in scenarios they might encounter. In each case, Bellagio management was acknowledging the vital importance of the frontline person's emotional state and the necessity of finding out how a candidate might behave in certain situations. A variety of approaches can be used to learn about the personality of a job candidate.

    A computer-driven system can also be used to create a master profile of the kind of person you want to hire. However you go about it, this much is certain: The mission is critical to the optimum presentation of the brand promise at the Human TouchPoint.

3. Managers know best. Why is the hiring process so problematic? Often because it is in the hands of an HR person who could never have as deep an understanding of the nuances of the job

that is being filled than the manager of that position. Bellagio's technological solution removed HR from the equation, replacing it with the managers most closely involved with any given job opening. As a result, the hotel has been able to field a better team for its Human TouchPoint.

The Container Store, incidentally, has followed a somewhat similar route, giving managers the responsibility for attracting, motivating, and retaining employees. The company is convinced that giving these tasks to managers clears the lines of communication, puts the decision-making responsibility where it belongs, and reduces turnover.

How to Hire the Right People

As the case studies in this chapter suggest, there is no one-size-fits-all personality type that is right for every company. Sure, intelligence and a courteous and respectful demeanor are critical when dealing face-to-face with your customers. But what other characteristics should you look for in a frontline hire? For one thing, you are not simply trying to find someone who will fit into your organization; the goal is to identify people who have the capacity to become outstanding, world-class performers. To achieve this goal you need a careful, analytical hiring policy.

I suggest you develop in-depth job-specific profiles of the kind of people you want at your Human TouchPoint. The frontline associate should be eager and capable of learning the job; the supervisor should be eager and capable of teaching and mentoring. In both cases, start by creating a master profile based on your current top performers. Use a computer-based behavioral profiling system, such as my TouchPoint Profile, to analyze both current employees and job candidates. Then compare the results of your job candidates with those of your top performers and include this data with personal interviews and other criteria in your overall assessment of the applicant.

The master profile will include standard information, such as education, work experience, and skill levels, but it should also pinpoint personal beliefs and attitudes. What a person thinks about herself is one example; what she's capable of learning to do is another. A candidate who considers herself good at math is more likely to develop better number-crunching capabilities than one who believes she is bad at math. By the same token, if a potential hire likes to try new things he's more likely to feel comfortable in a fast-changing organizational environment than would someone who prefers the familiar.

I have found over the years that people who have a talent for customer service have an innate desire to help others. When they help a customer find the right product or solve the customer's problem it actually gives them pleasure. And great customer-service managers are nurturing types who enjoy teaching and mentoring and who derive joy from others' successes. Such people are customer-service junkies; they are emotionally hooked on helping. They always need another customer to assist, much like an addict who always needs the next fix. Hiring people with these natural talents strengthens your Human TouchPoint because they require very little coaching to continue striving for excellence.

One often overlooked but essential part of the hiring process is to have the candidate preview the job slot. Make sure she is clear about the nature of the work and how she would spend her day. The more your new hire knows about the position the more likely you are to avoid the brisk employee turnover that kills customer satisfaction and corporate profitability. If she hates the idea of making collection calls to people in difficult financial straits and that is part of the job description she can turn down the position instead of quitting after she's been hired and trained.

Some companies present job candidates with descriptions of circumstances they will face and ask them to choose how they would cope from among several choices. Potential call-center operators are asked to listen to actual recorded customer calls and sort out their complaints. The candidates' untutored answers may reveal attitudes you should know about, but the point is to make the potential hires fully aware of what the job entails.

An area of particular concern involves the fit between a job candidate and the company's culture, either as it currently exists or as you envision it. Hiring the right people can help you build a stronger, more focused culture. If you plan to orient the culture more toward performance you will hire with that in mind. But to ensure that your new hire fits with your culture you must make the implicit explicit—by telling stories and setting context. When Starbucks trains its barista partners, for example, it starts with a lesson in Italian coffee culture. And when Blue Man trains new group members they learn the ideas and the moves that make a Blue Man performance unique.

Train Them the Right Way

No matter how thoroughly new hires have been briefed, no matter how carefully they've been tested, it's still a gamble. To hedge your bets, make absolutely certain that your new frontline employees are trained to excel at the Human TouchPoint. From what I've seen, most companies fail in this regard. Take United Airlines, for instance. United has one of the most famous, or perhaps I should say "infamous," brand promises: "Fly the friendly skies." But I can't tell you how often I have stood behind a United passenger coping with a surly gate agent or flight attendant—after which the passenger turned to me, rolled his or her eyes, and said, "Friendly skies . . . riiight!" In situations like this company leaders are typically shocked to discover that their frontline people are disconnected from the brand and have no sense of the customer perspective.

To guarantee that your frontline hires are primed for their positions define what the customer experience should look like, sound like, and feel like at each critical TouchPoint. Then define what role the frontline will play in fulfilling the promise. In other words, what should they be thinking, saying, and doing to create the desired customer experience?

To begin with, newcomers to your company need to understand how their assignment fits into the company's overall functioning. As in any organization, military or civilian, business success depends upon the actions of individual members of the group, and frontline people receive job satisfaction from knowing that everyone's efforts, up and down the supply chain, culminate in the frontline's job performance. The sales and service people are handed the product with the expectation that it will be presented appropriately to the customer. Frontline people should be made to appreciate that their performance will ultimately determine the size of everyone's paycheck as well as the company's fate. Anyone who cannot grasp the gravity of this responsibility should be reassigned or fired immediately.

New hires also need to be instructed about the why of their jobs—that is, the various contexts within which they will be operating: the competitive context, the environmental context, the departmental or divisional context, to name just a few. This understanding is what enables people to act appropriately. A failure to instill a companywide understanding of context is the most frequent problem I encounter among organizations.

In addition to context newcomers should be told how their commitment to excellence in customer service benefits the larger society. The company's raison d'être—to provide a product or service that improves people's lives while also making a profit—puts special emphasis on the frontline employee's importance.

The manager will want to make it clear from the beginning that she will coach the recruit to help him become a stellar performer. New hires represent an opportunity you cannot afford to miss. Whereas your veteran employees are entrenched in their particular jobs within the existing corporate culture the newcomers, by contrast, are open to fresh attitudes and goals. Take advantage of their malleability in your campaign to reinvigorate the culture and redesign the brand promise. And remember to provide as much positive reinforcement as possible. Managers should enjoy giving newcomers the support they need to maintain their self-esteem and develop pride in their work. Every effort should be made to inspire new people to believe in themselves and in their ability to achieve.

At the same time, new hires should be encouraged to think like owners, to take the initiative in looking for new and better ways to do their job—always with the understanding that they will not be punished or humiliated if such attempts fail. Familiarity with all of the culture's values is important for new hires, but you should emphasize that having positive interactions with customers is a special priority. A company dedicated to developing a peerless Human TouchPoint will not impede an employee's desire to help customers by imposing a rigid set of rules.

Now that you know how to find the right people and how to train them once they're hired, you are on your way to optimizing your Human TouchPoint. But I must add a caveat: No matter how well you do your job and how good your Human TouchPoint becomes at any given moment, you cannot afford to relax for long. Business is all about change. The only way to stay on top of the situation, to be sure that your frontline people are keeping their TouchPoints in tune with your brand promise, and that your brand promise is in tune with your market, is to continuously monitor both frontline people and their interactions with your customers.

Some years ago the leaders of Revco Drug Stores, which is now part of the CVS corporation, were determined to improve their Human TouchPoint, so they asked themselves: What do we want every customer to experience in every encounter he or she has with our stores? In other words, how can we promote better customer relations? The company's senior managers decided upon three very basic changes they wanted frontline people to make: These employees were to greet every customer entering a Revco store; they were to offer help to any customer searching for an item; and they were to look every customer in the eye when addressing him or her. The slogan for the new program was, appropriately enough, "Every customer, every time." Each store manager received a guide that suggested ways of effectively communicating the changes.

Weeks later Revco sent anonymous company shoppers to the stores to measure compliance with the new directive. The company also measured public reaction to the changes, keeping track of commendations and complaints from customers. Within a short time Revco found that compliance was averaging 90 percent, and the commendation/complaint ratio had tilted drastically toward commendation. The company made sure that the measures of customer reaction were shared with its frontline people to encourage them to persevere with the successful new approach. And, periodically, Revco repeated the same monitoring tactic.

Revco knew—and you should, too—that what happens at the Human TouchPoint is too important to leave to chance.

What's Next

No matter how you slice it, Human TouchPoints *are* unpredictable. But as the Blue Man Group, the Petty company, Edward Jones, and the other companies highlighted in this chapter prove, the right people with the proper training are irreplaceable in certain situations. And their unpredictability can even be an asset: Think of the Container Store employee who promptly took cash from the register to repay a customer for damage to her car. The frontline employee's quick—but unpredictable—reaction surely earned the gratitude and loyalty of a customer who might otherwise have waited weeks or months for reimbursement—if it ever came at all.

If your brand promise is one that would benefit from the human touch, my advice is to manage your frontline people carefully and use them wisely—just don't make the mistake of relying too heavily on an ultimately unreliable TouchPoint.

Some companies manage to achieve an almost perfect equilibrium among Product, System, and Human TouchPoints. The next chapter takes an up-close look at the secrets of an unrivaled champion of TouchPoint Branding: financial services retailer Washington Mutual. Washington Mutual brings to mind a beautifully engineered piece of machinery. It hums along from strength to strength, meshing its Product, System, and Human TouchPoints in a finely calibrated process that deftly fulfills its brand promise.

CHAPTER 8

A Case in TouchPoint:
Washington Mutual

ON A JUNE AFTERNOON in 1889, five Seattle, Washington, cabinetmakers panicked when a glue pot caught fire in their basement workshop at the corner of Front and Madison streets. One man threw water on the burning glue, spreading the flames throughout the shop. The cabinetmakers barely escaped to the street before fire engulfed the entire building. By the next morning Seattle's business district was in shambles. Twenty-nine blocks of wooden buildings, ten brick buildings, all but four of the city's wharves, and its railroad terminals were all destroyed. Miraculously, no lives were lost (unless you count the estimated one million roasted rats). Total reconstruction of the business district was the only choice.

Out of the ashes emerged a Runyonesque cast of characters. But one name stood out from the strivers and seekers: the Washington National Building Loan and Investment Association. Formed shortly after the great fire to help the city rebuild, Washington National was the only local source of construction loans for people with no assets. It was, in effect, an unbank marching to the beat of a civic-minded drummer. Within a year of the great fire Seattle's population had nearly doubled to forty-three thousand as a new city, the most glorious in the Pacific Northwest, emerged from a catastrophe that could easily have left nothing but ashes blowing in the wind.

The city's remarkable rebirth was followed by a difficult economic stretch at the turn of the century, but Washington National survived and prospered. Known for its innovation and generous withdrawal policies, accounts at the unbank grew sevenfold within five years. In 1917, the organization renamed itself the Washington Mutual Savings Bank.

Almost ninety years later Washington Mutual (affectionately shortened to WaMu) is still the customer-friendly unbank that competitors once disdained but now envy to the point of trying to imitate its distinct style coast to coast. They seldom succeed because WaMu is a study in contrast: a bank that makes big profits by totally banning every last vestige of the stereotypical big banker, that Scrooge in a suit who would evict his own mother if she missed one loan payment.

When you look at WaMu you see something different. When they go into the marketplace, they do so with a concentration of retail banking stores—retail settings that typically don't look like traditional banking branches. And they use very aggressive advertising, branding, and positioning with a twist.

WaMu's approach is simple: They have a straightforward brand promise they aggressively promote; their highly incentivized sales culture permeates the entire organization; they have the ability to drive in new consumer households through compelling products; and they have successful cross-sell programs, which in turn improve retention. Added to this is WaMu's commitment to streamline and simplify operations, pushing efficiencies and operational excellence throughout the company.

Customers are paying attention to this innovative financial services powerhouse. At the end of March 2003, WaMu served 7.6 million retail banking households through more than 1,700 retail banking stores and more than 3,000 ATMs.

Its signature markets, those where they have the full complement of its Consumer Group businesses, are in twenty-eight of the nation's top fifty markets. And in twelve of those markets WaMu maintains relationships with 30 percent or more of the consumer households.

The WaMu brand has helped build recognition in new markets, such as New York, and across distribution channels. It solidifies customer trust and loyalty and facilitates WaMu's in-store sales efforts. And they built it, in part, with creative advertising, resulting in number-one retail bank advertising awareness in key signature markets, including New York, Los Angeles, Miami, San Francisco, Seattle, and Houston.

WaMu has also been successful in expanding the number of households it serves through its lead checking account products. Since 2001, the number of retail checking accounts has grown 17 percent annually, primarily through internal growth.

So atypical is WaMu that new customers often hesitate, seemingly perplexed, when entering the bank's midtown Manhattan retail banking store on New York's famed Madison Avenue. Am I in the right place? Is this really a bank? A little confusion is understandable. A smiling concierge, soft lighting, and a comfortable waiting area greet customers at the door. There are no velvet ropes, no long counters with tellers behind bulletproof glass. Instead, casually dressed people stand in kiosks scattered around the room. Off to one side, in the WaMu Kids section, children are playing with Nintendo games.

But yes, this really is a serious bank—a branch of the nation's seventh-largest banking institution. From its Seattle headquarters, Washington Mutual oversees more than twenty-four hundred consumer banking, mortgage lending, commercial banking, and financial services offices throughout the nation. Determined to revolutionize its industry, it offers a new kind of banking experience, with all its TouchPoints carefully calibrated to underscore its banking innovations.

WaMu doesn't even want to be called a bank; by its own account it's a "retailer of financial services." But whatever you call it, the unbank business is a good one. Between 1997 and 2002, WaMu's earnings rose by an average of 34 percent a year, with net income reaching $3.86 billion by December 31, 2002. WaMu's profit continued to grow in 2003, but at a slower pace: Net income stood at $3.88 billion at the year's end.

WaMu's chief executive officer, Kerry Killinger, trades happily on the customer discontent fostered by competitors that herd customers into lines, apply rigid lending rules, close branches, charge for routine services, and try to avoid human contact with their clients. It's a kind of service that Brad Davis, executive vice president and chief marketing officer for WaMu, described to me as "the sound of a transaction happening." Nine times out of ten, in most stores, a transaction begins with the greeting: *"Next!"* That single word is one of the most damaging in retail. It says to the customer: "This is a *transaction,* and you are a *number."* How different is the experience when someone says: "Good Morning! How can I help!" That greeting is the beginning of a great customer experience, rather than just another transaction. What a difference! This focus on every detail of the customer experience is all part of the unbank notion that Killinger fosters. In fact, WaMu is the first major financial services company to commission J. D. Power and Associates to track their progress as they perfect their end-to-end methodology for managing the customer experience.

Killinger wants customers to think of WaMu as the place that says yes, and he aims to be a retailing category-killer on the scale of Wal-Mart, Home Depot, and Southwest Airlines.

When Killinger moved into the CEO's chair in 1990, WaMu's banking rivals were focused on courting wealthier clients with a hodgepodge of financial services. They also tried to cut costs by thinning out branch networks and pushing customers to bank via telephone, ATM, and computer. Killinger bucked the trend, emphasizing traditional branch banking and mortgage lending for all of WaMu's clients. WaMu's brand is decisively inclusive: "for everyone." So much so that the words are hardwired into their brand promise: "Great value with friendly service *for everyone.*" That means middle America and those who don't currently have a lot to invest. It's appealing. In a nation with a population growth of just 1 percent a year WaMu has managed to add customer households at an annual rate of 12 percent.

To compete with the big banks the CEO needed a larger platform. He launched a decade-long series of acquisitions, ultimately acquiring more than thirty regional banks, mortgage lenders, and brokers. By 2002, when WaMu entered New York City in a $5.2 billion purchase of the 126-branch Dime Savings Bank, total assets had grown tenfold, to $275 billion. The number of employees had shot up to 52,500 in 2002 from 2,100 in 1990, and WaMu had emerged as the nation's largest servicer of mortgages, with a $770 billion portfolio.

Killinger made sure the acquisitions were efficiently integrated into the Washington Mutual corporate culture, and he never let growth-by-acquisition become a substitute for internal expansion. From the beginning of 2000 to the end of 2002, more than four million customers switched to WaMu and the company added eight hundred thousand checking accounts to its base in 2003 alone.

Now that WaMu has achieved considerable mass, growth will primarily be internal.

Recognizing that to keep the momentum going customer service has to be its number-one priority, WaMu makes sure its service is second to none by consciously focusing on its Product Touch-Points, System TouchPoints, and Human TouchPoints. As a result, WaMu is fulfilling its unique brand promise in ways that make customers (and competitors) take notice.

WaMu's Product TouchPoints

WaMu believes that for consumers, personal checking accounts and home loans are their two most important financial relationships. If WaMu can "own" these relationships, then they have a great chance to keep the household long term and improve their ability to cross sell other products and services.

WaMu is a research-driven organization that conducts multiple field studies every business day. In 2003, WaMu surveyed more than one million consumers. WaMu's research showed that customers were irritated by the "nickel and dime fees" associated with other banks' checking accounts, so they invented totally free checking—with no minimum balance, no monthly fee, no per-check charges, no direct deposit requirement, no charge to access WaMu's national ATM network, and no fee to talk to a teller.

Free checking and home loans offer excellent opportunities for cross selling additional consumer deposits and loans over time. When free checking is the entry product for new households WaMu is able to grow deposit, investment, mortgage, and consumer loan balances in subsequent years to reach around twenty-five thousand dollars at the end of five years. The same can be said when home loans are the lead product: Other account balances grow to approximately fifteen thousand dollars over the same period.

Killinger defies conventional wisdom by successfully branding his mortgages. Most bankers think brand doesn't matter, because mortgages are a commodity that trades on price alone. WaMu differentiates its mortgages by stressing accessibility and service. "Consumers want to feel trust and stability when they think of their mortgage company," one executive told me, "because this one transaction has such a huge impact on their lives." A brand, this executive believes, goes far beyond clever ads and slogans: "A successful brand is a reflection of everything a company is; it reflects the heart and soul of a company."

And just as with free checking a WaMu mortgage is only an introduction to other WaMu Product TouchPoints. If they don't already have one the next step is usually a free checking account. This, in turn, can lead to a mutual fund purchase, an insurance policy, an auto loan, an education loan, or a bit further down the road, a home-equity loan.

Since 2001, the bank has offered a "platinum account"—a premium checking account that pays competitive money market interest rates for balances of twenty-five thousand dollars. In its first thirty months the platinum account brought in fifty billion dollars in new deposits.

WaMu's studies have shown that the more Product TouchPoints it offers the more customers will use, and clients who cross buy products and services are more likely to stay with the bank. After one year, 96.5 percent of clients using four WaMu products are still customers, while only 75.5 percent of those using just one service continue to bank at WaMu.

Clearly, WaMu's Product TouchPoints are aligned with its brand promise in a way that makes the vast majority of the bank's customers unusually receptive to expanding the relationship.

WaMu's System TouchPoints

In a made-in-heaven marriage of TouchPoints WaMu uses a System TouchPoint, its technology, to enhance and support its Product TouchPoint.

WaMu is carefully tuning its System TouchPoints to make the customer's banking experience as smooth and consistent as possible. The goal is to make it easy for people to do business with WaMu no matter how they choose to do it—by phone, online, or in an office. What is more, WaMu's technology is designed to provide plenty of room for variation where it counts. Unlike banks that dictate every move from headquarters, WaMu gives its retail banking store managers considerable autonomy, so that a store in Florida, say, can have a product and staffing mix that stresses checking accounts, while a store in Seattle emphasizes home equity loans. The processes and systems across the country mesh seamlessly and consistently. The company's Web site, for instance, reflects WaMu's signature brand of retail banking, which is a dramatic shift from traditional bank branches in look, feel, and service. In other words, the company takes pains to ensure that the level of service online (or through its customer call centers) is just as friendly and efficient as it is in the branches.

The call centers are kept open seven days a week, twenty-four hours a day, and this System TouchPoint, too, is carefully tended. Originally, customers' calls were routed to the team that granted their loan. But the system sometimes experienced overloads, causing customers to endure long waits. A load-balancing feature was added, routing calls to whichever center is least busy. Reduced waiting time makes for happier customers.

The supporting technology for System TouchPoints focuses, as it should, on the customers. But WaMu also makes sure to include its partners—Realtors, brokers, the capital markets, and other banks whose loans WaMu services. The bank's home loans group maintains business-to-business Web sites that help its partners serve their customers faster and more flexibly. One such site, www-.premierebroker.com, allows Washington Mutual brokers to submit applications and receive loan approvals and other information online. Another site, www.wamumsc.com, provides more effective and consistent communication with investors, servicers, and sellers.

The first System TouchPoint most customers encounter is the bank's marketing, especially in areas where WaMu is not already well known. Here the bank is inventive and thoroughly uninhibited, appealing to its targeted customers—individual consumers and small business, or those "everyday people" who make up most of the population—with outdoor barbecues, live music, and community events that support teachers, education, and affordable housing.

A three-month marketing blitz accompanied WaMu's New York market entry after the Dime Savings acquisition. It was designed to win recognition and establish a presence in a hip, blasé market then dominated by Chase and Citigroup. One part of the campaign set out to thank the city's schoolteachers by recognizing them with a program called Spotlight on Teachers. The three-month promotion culminated on a Saturday in November, with WaMu treating more than twenty-eight thousand New York– and New Jersey–area teachers and their guests to a Broadway performance, complete with a ticker-tape send-off in Shubert Alley. The unprecedented move, in which WaMu bought out every available seat for the matinee performances, was the largest single buy-out in Broadway history. Further showcasing the bank's uniquely innovative style, twenty-nine stage-struck teachers got to act out their dreams in bit parts. Among the twenty-nine was Lillian Hopkins, who teaches eighth grade at the Rocco Laurie Middle School on Staten Island. She danced that afternoon in the chorus of *Thoroughly Modern Millie* in a theater on Shubert Alley. "It was a once-in-a-lifetime event," she gushed to *Fast Company*.

Like Spotlight on Teachers, the introductory marketing campaigns are tailored to each individual market. WaMu's advertising in the Big Apple, for instance, had a New York edge. Eye-catching subway posters announced "a small revolution in banking." Newspaper ads proclaimed "The end of minimum balance oppression" and showed jubilant customers in fighting poses wearing novelty-store goggles.

Perhaps the ultimate symbol of all of WaMu's TouchPoints, however, is yet another System TouchPoint: the look and feel of WaMu's retail banking stores. WaMu has always believed in offering banking services to people in branches. In the late 1990s, while other banks were directing customers to their ATMs or debating

clicks versus bricks, WaMu was pioneering a new way to bring consumer banking to the next level. WaMu launched its new signature
brand of retail banking in April 2001 after nearly two years of intensive customer research into every Product, System, and Human
TouchPoint in the typical bank. Every feature was thought through
and tested, from the children's play area, to the concierge who
greets customers and guides them to the services they need, to the
"teller towers," which allow the WaMu sales associate to conduct
business without counting or distributing cash. WaMu employees
serve customers side by side at the teller towers, which are placed
in a circular formation in the main area of the store. No glass or
iron barriers separate the employee from the customer, which
helps provide a more welcoming environment to conduct business and allows the employee to focus on providing face-to-face,
friendly service. By eliminating the high counters, buttoned-down
clerks, and impersonal service often associated with banking
WaMu has created a retail environment where people want to go,
rather than have to go. As an executive of a leading retail association commented, WaMu has taken an industry that was once considered staid and has successfully infused it with a customer-centric
retail environment, creating a model for other financial institutions
as well as for other retailers. No wonder WaMu was once named
one of the top forty stores in the world by the International Mass
Retailing Association.

By the end of 2004, WaMu expects to have opened a total of 637
new retail banking stores since it first began rolling out the new retail store model in 2000. And this includes 230 new stores in 2003
and another 250 scheduled for 2004.

Even the design of some WaMu offices, which customers never
see, have been tailored to make the bank's processes and systems
run smoother and more efficiently. Individual space for these
staffers has been reduced, but there is more common space, which
promotes collaboration. People have impromptu meetings in areas

furnished with lounge chairs and movable whiteboards suspended from the ceiling. They meet and talk over complimentary coffee and tea in the café. The concept is called a village because it has the features of a neighborhood—a café, copy center, post office, library, and conference center. As Kent Wiegel, senior vice president of corporate property services, told *Building Operating Management:* "We think this is the office of the future. The energy level is higher, communication is better because people can see each other more easily, and we've been able to cut the cost to house a typical administrative employee by at least 20 percent."

WaMu's Human TouchPoints

Banking is relationships, and for all the latter-day emphasis on cost-cutting via ATMs and online banking, the relationships that matter most are invariably human. No one knows this better than WaMu, and the bank's corporate culture is relentless in its determination to create Human TouchPoints that back up the promise of its brand.

To that end, in 2002 Killinger named seventy-five "brand ambassadors," who represent every region and product line, to promote the corporate culture among all of WaMu's employees. An estimated 40,000 employees have taken brand training classes, and nearly 50 brand rallies have been held for up to 1,000 employees at a time.

As WaMu's chief "brand ambassador," Killinger has met personally with nearly half of the workforce, either when he led brand rallies or in one-on-one talks. Additionally, he holds an annual "state of the group" conference for thirty-five hundred of the bank's cheering, fist-pumping senior managers, and he is so successful at promoting the corporate culture that critics say it verges on a cult. The bank's employees even call themselves "WaMulians"—as in, "Hi, I'm Kevin. I'm a WaMulian from Consumer Lending."

Fortune magazine has recognized WaMu as one of the "100 Best

Companies to Work For" and one of "America's Best Companies for Minorities" while *Executive FEMALE* magazine named WaMu one of its "Top 30 Companies for Executive Women."

Killinger himself is praised by Wall Street—especially since the collapse of the dot-com bubble—for what one analyst calls his "flamboyance vacuum." The son of an Iowa music teacher, Killinger is quiet and matter-of-fact, with an everyday-Joe touch that appeals to his target customers: He once conducted merger negotiations while knocking out a wall to accommodate his new freezer. He went through undergraduate and graduate business school at the University of Iowa in just four years, raising money by buying and fixing up homes for rent or sale. His prize deal: He bought a house for $3,700, put $4,000 into it (he personally dug the foundation), and sold it for $22,000.

As Killinger sees it, WaMu's Human TouchPoints begin with hiring for attitude and finding the right people—and they're found at least as often in retailing as in the banking field. They find it easier to redesign stuffy branch offices and hire smiling concierges.

Outside-the-vault thinking is a perfect way to describe how Brad Davis approaches his job. Davis, who, incidentally, came to WaMu from the retailing field, knows that marketing magic comes not from a well-drawn set of advertising plans but from the way they're executed. "Brands come alive operationally, in the people," he told me, and people come alive through what he likes to call "myth and mythology," or storytelling.

To that end, Davis shuns the typical corporate reliance on memos as a prime means of communication: "You can put a document together and distribute it to fifty thousand people, and it'll end up turning yellow pinned up on someone's tackboard. That's not going to work." Instead, he inculcates troops in the WaMu way by telling stories of good and bad behavior. His "sound of a transaction happening" story, for example, has been told and retold in the WaMu ranks, passed along as received wisdom. He says it's about imparting your message "in living color." That way people remember it and internalize it. They never even have to think about how the company wants them to behave; it's become a natural part of them. That's how, in his words, you deliver the "ideal customer experience."

CEO Killinger also thinks it's vital to convey the WaMu attitude and culture immediately and emphatically to employees who come on board as part of an acquisition. After the Dime Savings purchase, for instance, there was no "transition period" from the Dime brand to the WaMu culture. Instead, Killinger rented the Hammerstein Theater on West 34th Street and treated three thousand Dime employees to a two-hour indoctrination in the WaMu way of life. For hard-bitten New Yorkers it amounted to culture shock—a two-hour dunking in down-home fun and niceness. But Killinger's message came through loud and clear, and the former Dime branches began the WaMu life then and there.

As with the intertwined nature of Product and System Touch-Points, so too the Human TouchPoints. The technology supporting and enhancing WaMu's Human TouchPoints helps tellers and loan officers get a full profile of each client, enabling them to make fast, accurate decisions.

In the years to come Killinger wants WaMu to be a leader in three key areas: retail banking, home lending, and lending to apartment and condominium developers.

WaMu innovation is rapidly becoming the stuff of urban legend, helped along by such things as innovative partnerships with Magic Johnson's Johnson Development Corporation, an established leader in serving ethnic minority markets. Additionally, as part of *Fortune's* "2004 Most Admired Companies," WaMu was selected as the most innovative company in the country in any industry, beating out such venerable organizations as Starbucks, Procter & Gamble, UPS, and Nike.

Very soon WaMu will be perceived not as a bank, the CEO maintains, but as the leading retailer of financial services. And after that, who knows? As he told *Fortune,* Killinger believes that every five years "you have to reinvent your company and become completely different."

That's a tall order, but the WaMu chief already has a wealth of success under his belt. For most people, banking has always been a chore. By rethinking all of the bank's TouchPoints to maximize consistency and reinforce its unique brand promise, WaMu has crafted a warm and inviting retail experience that customers actually enjoy. Indeed, so comfortable is this experience that one elderly Florida woman spends part of every day in the lobby of her WaMu retail banking store. She knits, greets customers, and engages them in pleasant conversation. Having been made to feel welcome herself by the branch manager and other employees, she returns the favor by helping her WaMu friends deliver friendly service to others.

Reveling in telling me this story, Brad Davis captured the essence of WaMu itself when he praised that branch manager as "one of my heros . . . the living personification of our brand." Why? Because the manager made the brand promise come alive when he encouraged what is surely an atypical retail customer relationship. And, as Davis points out, living the brand can pay great rewards: I wouldn't be surprised if this customer is asking everybody in town, "Want a friendly bank? Go to WaMu!"

This is a company that is delivering on its brand promise, providing value and excellent service in a friendly and, yes, caring fashion. And happy customers make for happy shareholders: *Forbes* named Washington Mutual as one of the fifty most profitable companies in the world. From the end of 1990 through the end of 2003 WaMu's stock price, adjusted for stock splits, has risen from $0.024 a share to $40.12 a share.

CHAPTER 9

A Case in TouchPoint:
Lexus

A NAME CAN BE a single syllable or a complex list describing origins, occupations, or even birth order. But whether one word or many, names help define us and serve to distinguish one person from another. And as every boy named Sue would surely attest, names can influence not only the way others see us, but also the way we see ourselves. In short, personal names can pack a powerful punch. So, too, for automobiles.

Names are a critical Product TouchPoint that begins to define the emotional bond a car's owners will feel for it. Traditional brands like Ford, Chrysler, and Buick began with the founder's name and acquired emotional resonance over the years. But modern nameplates tend to be a made-up string of syllables that together evoke a feeling—hopefully the one the creators had in mind! Chevrolet named its Nova to signify new and brilliant. Unfortunately, Spanish-speaking drivers translated Nova as "It doesn't go."

Aware of the pitfalls Toyota's managers spent weeks pondering a list of 219 names dreamed up by Lippincott & Margulies, a New York image consultant, for the new luxury car model the Japanese carmaker was going to debut in 1989. The suggestions ranged from Calibre and Chaparel to Vectre and Verone, but the emerging favorite was Alexis. At a marketing meeting in Los Angeles, however, then corporate marketing manager George Borst pointed out that Alexis was the name of the demanding diva played by Joan Collins in *Dynasty*, a popular television series of the day. With that, John French, project manager for the car, began to doodle the name on a notepad, minus the A. The spelling soon evolved from Lexis to Lexus, suggesting both the Latin *luxus* (luxury) and the French *luxe* (sumptuous). The result was a brilliant invention that perfectly evoked the image they were seeking—a new, more contemporary expression of luxury.

By the time the car was named, however, it had already traveled a long road. The journey began early in 1983 when Yuki Togo, head of Toyota Motor's U.S. division, flew to Tokyo to try to persuade the company's directors to enter the luxury car market. A victory in that hotly contested field, Togo argued, could position Toyota as a leader in the whole U.S. market. And "if [we] could earn the badge of 'No. 1' in this huge market," Togo went on, "it would send reverberations throughout the world."

The board members weren't easily sold. They had qualms about taking on the high-end European automakers who had been operating in the U.S. market for years. Worse, they worried that a successful challenge to the American leaders, Cadillac and Lincoln, might embroil Toyota in regulatory trade disputes with Washington. At bottom, though, the directors feared the project would undermine Toyota's corporate mission, which had been to build cars for the masses. "The third of Toyota's five guiding precepts was 'Be practical and avoid frivolity,'" Togo recalls. Would a luxury car damage the image of a people's car company?

Togo made several transpacific flights to build a constituency for his idea. He argued that the move was essentially the logical outcome of Kiichiro Toyoda's bold step fifty years earlier, when he led his father's loom and textile machinery company into the automotive age despite a foreboding history of Japanese failures in the field. Eventually, then chairman Eiji Toyoda, Kiichiro's cousin, gave Togo the nod at the August board meeting. "It is time," he said, "to build a car that is better than the best in the world." Toyoda was committing his company to building not just a viable luxury car for the American market, but an automotive experience that would trump the luxury status quo—Jaguar, BMW, and Mercedes.

A fifteen-man planning committee was named, and its marching orders were sweeping. The car, code-named Circle F for flagship, would be a closely guarded secret whose research and development would take years. It would not be built on the cheap, using an existing Toyota platform; rather, it would be new from the wheels up. No limits were placed on either the time or money devoted to it. That commitment was vital, for when you set out to be the best, you must be ready to do whatever it takes to get there.

Equally important, the project began with the kind of disciplined market research that is essential to effective TouchPoint Branding. In a simple yet breathtaking approach Toyota decided that to build a luxury car for the U.S. market it first had to understand what is unique about the concept of luxury in America. The Japanese precept of *genchi genbutsu*—go look, go see—became its guide.

In April 1985, a team of twenty designers and engineers flew off to begin a total immersion in luxurious American living, with orders from Togo to learn everything they could about the life and values of high-end buyers. "You cannot create a 'child of America' unless you understand Americans," he said. "What does a car mean to them? How do they use it? How do they feel when they ride in a car? How does a well-to-do lady get into an automobile with her fur coat on?"

Moving into a large house overlooking the ocean at Laguna Beach, California, an hour south of Los Angeles, the team began a five-month quest. They visited country clubs, upscale malls, youth soccer leagues, and chic restaurants. They saw men tossing golf bags into Jaguars, women ferrying kids in Benzes and Volvos, and valets parking exotic sports cars. The men from Japan were astonished: "Otherwise respectable people in L.A. drove cars that would have branded them as members of the underworld in Japan," Togo explained. But gradually they began to understand how the U.S. luxury market had evolved from the flamboyance of the fifties through the counterculture of the sixties and the pendulum's return swing in the eighties. Hippies and antiwar protesters had morphed into yuppies and advertising executives, and conspicuous consumption was no longer taboo—far from it. *Newsweek* magazine, in a 1984 cover story headlined, "The Year of the Yuppie," called it, "a new plane of consciousness, a state of Transcendental Acquisition."

The Toyota team fanned out to observe focus groups of luxury consumers in San Francisco, Denver, Houston, New York, and Miami. In suburban Chicago they videotaped a wealthy woman as she walked through her home describing her tastes and values, and again as she drove her Jaguar through her community and talked about her neighbors, their houses, and their customs. The tape was played in Japan for hundreds of Toyota designers and engineers. Finally, a consensus was reached: The taste of the American luxury consumer was basically European, but brighter, warmer, and more approachable.

The team returned to Japan, except for five designers who stayed behind in California to begin building clay models of the Lexus. "We couldn't have designed this car in Japan and made it look the way we wanted it to look in America," said Kunihiro Uchida, who oversaw the car's exterior design. "Buildings, the width of streets, other cars on the road, even the vegetation . . . they all affect how a car looks."

Initially, the design team was a bit daunted by the competition. Jaguar, BMW, and Mercedes had recently established solid beachheads in a market long dominated by Lincoln and Cadillac, gaining cachet among more sophisticated buyers who viewed the American offerings as somewhat bulgy and overstuffed, certainly not nimble. The Europeans had exploited the chinks in the American armor, and Toyota wondered how it might compete against the hardcharging invaders.

Auto-industry shoptalk provided at least a partial answer. For years insiders had wisecracked that luxury-car drivers had to "suffer the badge," meaning that if they wanted the brand's prestige they had to endure the mechanical shortcomings of the cars and the snobbish attitude of the dealers, who patronized customers and provided slow, offhand service. Early on, Lexus decided it would exploit these weaknesses. Flawless performance (a Product Touch-Point) and an unprecedented level of personal service (a Human TouchPoint) would be key elements of the Lexus brand promise.

The promise to be "better than the best in the world" was first roughed out by Eiji Toyoda. But one day in 1987, two full years before the first Lexus appeared in a showroom, general manager Dave Illingworth dictated an inspired refinement of Toyoda's order that became the Lexus covenant. Now it's carved in granite at the division's headquarters and etched into the frontal lobe of every Lexus manager, salesperson, and mechanic:

> Lexus will enter the most competitive, prestigious automobile race in the world. Over 50 years of Toyota automotive experience has culminated in the creation of Lexus cars. They will be the finest cars ever built.
>
> Lexus will win the race because: Lexus will do it right from the start. Lexus will have the finest dealer network in the industry. Lexus will treat each customer as we would a guest in our home.
>
> If you think you can't, you won't. If you think you can, you will. We can, we will.

"The finest cars in the world . . . do it right from the start . . . treat each customer as we would a guest in our home." All of that is summed up in the Lexus brand promise: the passionate pursuit of perfection. And by translating that passionate pursuit into a series of Product, System, and Human TouchPoints, Lexus has achieved perfect success.

Product TouchPoints, the Lexus Way

It's obvious that Lexus has kept its brand promise. Sales soared steadily from 16,000 units in 1989, its first year on the market, to 260,000 units in 2003, when it was the top-selling luxury nameplate in the United States for the fourth year in a row. Its claim to be the finest car in the world is backed up by an endless string of awards from the automotive press; the prestigious J. D. Power & Associates ranked it number one in long-term dependability for six straight years and number one in customer satisfaction for seven of the past eight years. From Lexus's own viewpoint, however, the most telling measure is its success in beating the Europeans: In the brand's first two years fully 45 percent of its customers traded in a European car for their new Lexus. The figure has dropped since then, but mainly because Lexus retains 53 percent of its customers—the highest loyalty rate of any nameplate. No wonder BMW, Jaguar, and Mercedes are on the defensive.

The first reason for the Lexus's success, of course, is the product itself and the string of TouchPoints that define it. Among them is an innovation that came from a member of the initial design team, Michikazu Masu. Masu's daughter, who rode in a carpool to her California school, asked him why she slid forward in her seat every time her classmate's mother hit the brakes of her Mercedes. Masu immediately realized that the interiors of German cars were too stiff. If riding in a Cadillac was like sinking into a divan, riding in a Mercedes was like sitting in a stiff-backed chair. Lexus could exploit this weakness in European design by finding middle ground.

Another epiphany came when Masu held a garage sale and discovered that the upscale buyers were more intrigued by the map to his house than by the merchandise. The visitors praised the map he had drawn as "simple, clean, and smart." Masu would not have used those words to describe the luxury-car market, but now he thought otherwise. Simple, clean, and smart became the Lexus watchwords for key design features, large and small.

For customers, Lexus's first Product TouchPoint is the feeling they get when they slide behind the wheel—the unspoken "aah" that comes with experiencing a long dreamed of height of luxury. That feeling is reinforced by a wealth of subtle details, ranging from buttery-soft leather seats and the rich gleam of the wood-trimmed interior to the Lexus's hushed, silky ride and smooth handling. All of these details are the product of never-ending questioning, research, testing, and reworking. Nothing is too small to escape notice. When Toyota's interior designers were testing different steering wheels, for example, they bought plastic press-on fingernails to get a sense of how American women might experience various design options. The same level of interest and intensity goes into every square inch of every Lexus, inside and out.

Lexus pursues perfection just as painstakingly when it comes to the actual production of its cars. Production workers in Japan are empowered to halt the line at the least hint of a problem, from a dropped screwdriver to a bulging seam in a car's upholstery. And Lexus managers boast that production won't resume until the problem is fixed, no matter whether it takes seconds or minutes. A sure sign of Lexus's unwavering commitment to quality came in the first months of production in 1988, when cars began arriving in California with noisy fan belts. Another company might well have decided to fix the problem on the fly, continuing production, shipping the cars, and replacing the defective parts at the dealerships. But Lexus is not just another car company. It stopped the line and shipped no cars from Japan until their belts were quiet.

Market research is a key driver of all Lexus Product TouchPoints. The division keeps in touch with its customers through focus groups, surveys, and studies conducted by in-house and outside specialists. Lexus managers like to say that other companies build cars to satisfy engineers; they build cars to give contemporary buyers the perfect luxury experience.

And over time the car's Product TouchPoints have evolved to

reflect both the customers' changing tastes and the company's widening range of product choices. From its original LS 400 model, Lexus has grown to an eight-model line that ranges from quietly luxurious to performance-oriented. Models were developed for the entry- and mid-level-luxury buyers as well as for bigger spenders. The 1998 GS, the world's fastest automatic-transmission sedan, was produced as a head-on challenge to BMW, and Lexus gave birth to the luxury crossover market with its first SUV, the RX 300. Named *Motor Trend* magazine's sport utility of the year when it was introduced in 1998, the RX 300 quickly became a market leader. Lexus recently introduced the RX 400h, the world's first luxury hybrid SUV powered by gasoline-electric technology. Its 270-horsepower, V-6 engine muscles the car from 0 to 60 miles per hour in less than 8 seconds, while also generating electric power for cruising that makes the RX 400h's fuel efficiency comparable to that of a compact sedan. Fuel efficiency is a powerful TouchPoint for today's socially conscious buyers. As an environmental bonus, the hybrid's emissions, which are among the lowest in the industry, give it the rating of a Super Ultra Low Emission Vehicle (SULEV). Finally, a guilt-free SUV that also boasts unequaled performance, safety, and luxury features.

As its cars have evolved, so has the Lexus brand. The changes have been subtle, and in harmony with the changes in the market and the Lexus Product TouchPoints. With the introduction of the GS and RX 300, for instance, Lexus modified its slogan. A pursuit of perfection once proclaimed as "relentless" now became "passionate." As befits a car company born of a command "to be better than the best" Lexus understands that brand promises cannot remain static; they must be constantly managed, evaluated, and adapted to keep step with changes in the marketplace, your company, and the world at large. Lexus's choice of the word "passionate" is a bid to infuse the brand with more emotion, in line with its new emphasis on the vehicles' performances and the excitement they ignite. The change indicates to customers that they can now expect even more than what they were typically used to from Lexus.

From the cars' accessories to the tenor of the advertising, everything denoting the brand has evolved in lockstep. At its launch, the perfection of the Lexus signified that the buyer was making a rational choice to own a car without flaws. Now that perfection signifies not just the absence of defects but the unspoiled fun of active enjoyment. When the speedy GS was introduced, for instance, the headline on its first ad was mischievous: "Something Wicked This Way Comes." Lexus always offered a perfectly quiet interior cabin but now, with the addition of a top-quality Mark Levinson sound system, the Lexus driver could infuse that perfect quiet with the perfect sound of her favorite symphony. And Lexus ads told buyers that they would be "catered to, protected, indulged . . . to make your trip more pleasurable."

The brand has been enhanced and supported in other ways, too. Early on, as a way to introduce the car to customers, Lexus marketed to rental companies. But in 1995, when the managers decided that fleet sales weren't good for resale values, customer satisfaction, or the basic luxury image, they cut off a source of sales that had grown to ten thousand cars a year. Overall sales volume dropped that year, but so what? Volume, Lexus declared, is not what drives a luxury brand. The sales would come back from sources that were more solid—and so they did.

I've seen other brands make this kind of rolling readjustment, but I've never seen anyone do it better than Lexus.

System TouchPoints, the Lexus Way

From the beginning Lexus designed its System TouchPoints to make sure customers had a flawless experience every time they interacted with the company, particularly when their cars needed servicing. Lexus's European competitors at the high end of the auto market were especially vulnerable when it came to service, as "suffering the badge" often meant chronic breakdowns, days waiting for parts, the discomfort of driving a rattletrap "loaner" car, or even having to rent a replacement. And rubbing salt in the wound were dealers who merely shrugged when customers complained.

To exploit this weakness among its rivals Lexus management recognized early on that a network of superior dealers would be the carmaker's most important System TouchPoint. Fortunately, Toyota's reputation for quality drew hundreds of dealer applications when word spread that it was planning a luxury car. Lexus made the prospect even more enticing by offering unprecedented levels of support. To ensure profitability it kept the number of dealers below one hundred at the car's launch, and just about double that figure at full production. Lexus picks up the cost of training mechanics to make sure they know the car inside out, and the company's top executives regularly meet with Lexus dealers to guarantee that the dealers have an active voice in the company.

Among Lexus's first batch of dealers, 90 percent came from the top drawer of existing Toyota dealers. The others were seasoned dealers who had earned outstanding reputations with rival brands. All the new dealers were given tours of the Lexus design and production facilities and indoctrinated in the Lexus philosophy, and all of them signed the Lexus covenant.

The dealerships themselves have been designed to convey solid luxury and to appeal strongly to the targeted buyers. However, this System TouchPoint got off to a shaky start when, two years before the launch, Bob McCurry, Toyota executive vice president, snorted that the building design looked "like a Kentucky Fried Chicken" outlet. That's when Dave Illingworth recruited Jim Sherburne from the Toyota design studio in Newport Beach, California. Inspired by the serenity and strength of Japanese gardens, Sherburne came up with a distinctly untrendy design for a building with a stone facade above a smooth expanse of glass and a stone pillar at each end. To convey integrity and reliability, the look extends to all sides of the building. The Lexus logo is on the left of the facade, and the dealership's name on the right. The size and style of lettering are restricted and no tacky banners or pennants are visible. In addition, the stone for the facades comes in three shades of grayish tan—a cool one for conservative locations, a slightly warmer, lighter shade for less formal places, and an even warmer sandy color for Lexus dealerships in the Southwest.

Sherburne's vision also extended into the showroom, where coffee tables and leather chairs create a comfortable space for sales representatives to confer with customers. "When you're sitting down around a coffee table, everybody's equal," he explains. There are also comfortable lounges where customers can wait while their cars are being serviced. To make customers feel like guests in a private home some waiting lounges even include fireplaces. No design detail of this System TouchPoint was overlooked. In the service department, for instance, the write-up area is positioned next to the driveway. When a customer drives in a technician can punch the license plate number into the computer and have the car's history on the screen by the time the customer walks through the door—to be greeted by name.

Many of the features stemmed from an internal research project organized by Dick Chitty, corporate manager for parts and service. Chitty instructed his staff to spend a couple of days writing down every complaint about auto service they had ever heard. The chief complaint turned out to be that owners generally have no idea what mechanics do to their cars. More than half of Mercedes owners, Chitty learned, go to independent shops for service—and not because dealer service is too pricey, or even because of a lack of convenience. Rather, "they wanted to talk to the person who was going to work on their car," Chitty said. So Lexus converted its senior mechanics into "diagnostic specialists" who wear white shirts and tell the customers what's going on. And the service bays are visible from the lounge through a wall of windows, so customers can watch their cars being worked on—"like fathers looking in at their newborns," as Sherburne puts it.

But when all is said and done, the dealers have to grasp just one principle, says Illingworth: "Take care of each customer one at a time." People try to make the auto business very complicated, he says, "but I think, in reality, it's very simple. You just do [that] one thing . . . [and] you'll be just fine."

Of course, the Lexus definition of how to take care of customers goes well beyond the industry standard. For instance, the first two scheduled maintenance visits are free, and any car that comes in for service is washed before it goes back to the owner. If service takes more than a day the customer gets a loaner car free of charge—and the loaner is a Lexus, not some beat-up compact. The icing on the cake of this extraordinary System TouchPoint: Lexus buyers receive a complimentary twenty-four-hour roadside assistance program that covers the costs, if necessary, of a rental car, a hotel room, and up to three days' worth of meals.

Now you understand why Lexus continues to rack up those J. D. Power customer satisfaction ratings. The company has the industry's best record in dealer servicing: Fully 64 percent of Lexus cars on the road for ten years or less are maintained by Lexus dealers. What is more, this horde of satisfied customers has put Lexus at the top of the industry, along with Toyota, in sales per dealership—not to mention having the industry's happiest and most profitable dealers.

Still, it's not enough. Like any good TouchPoint Brander, Lexus management knows it must constantly renew and upgrade its System TouchPoints as its brand evolves and conditions change. So, in October of 2002, a number of Lexus officials set out on a multicity New Luxury Tour of the United States. The goal: to instill in dealers and associates across the country a new awareness of Lexus's expanded brand promise, and to invite them to suggest new and better System TouchPoints.

The tour was never intended as a way to bring marching orders to the troops. Instead, the headquarters team wanted to hear people's ideas and tap into solutions that fit their particular operations—ideas and solutions that might or might not be adapted for use by dealers in other markets. Lexus values the input of its dealers, and its aim was to build on existing strengths to reach higher levels of excellence.

The effort paid off. For one thing, a massive investment is being made to upgrade systems. In the past two years Lexus dealers have put a total of five hundred million dollars into improving their facilities. And the individual initiatives have been both bold and creative. A dealer in Michigan, for example, installed a marble cappuccino bar in his customer lounge. The aroma alone is a System TouchPoint that says "welcome," and customers now have reason to actually enjoy the time they spend there. A dealer in Las Vegas invited high-end retailer Neiman Marcus to open a boutique for customers in his lounge, while the Carlsbad, California, dealership turned its customer lounge into a virtual home away from home, complete with marble and wood trim. Waiting customers can watch television on big-screen plasma TVs, view fine artwork, sip cappuccino, and munch pastries, or plug into any of eight Internet stations at the coffee bar or two more in private booths at the back. If customers can work productively at the dealership, says general manager Gene Manganiello, they don't have to waste time driving back and forth to the office. It's also just a nice place to spend time. "I overheard one customer telephoning a friend to come join her in our lounge because she was so impressed with the facility," says Manganiello.

And in the New York City exurbs of northern New Jersey the New Luxury Tour inspired dealer Ray Catena to revolutionize his entire sales process, streamlining it to eliminate pressure on the customers and reduce hassle in the dealing. He has hired several product specialists who are far removed from the stereotypical car salesman: college-educated, salaried professionals who wander around the showroom floor providing detailed information about the cars and their features, and answering questions for browsing customers. Only when the customer expresses a definite interest in buying does the product specialist walk him or her over for an introduction to a sales consultant who will write up the deal.

The Lexus System TouchPoints are flexible and varied, but they all work to support the brand's prime goal: ensuring a smooth and comfortable experience for the customer.

Human TouchPoint, the Lexus Way

As with most luxury products the Human TouchPoint is crucial to Lexus's success. Human contact is inevitable in selling and servicing cars, and it has to be pleasant, courteous, attentive, and responsive to a customer's every need if Lexus is to satisfy and retain its targeted buyers. So the company's Human TouchPoint starts from the top: Many new owners get a personal call from an employee at the company's United States headquarters in Torrance, California, welcoming the buyer to the Lexus family and making sure everything about the purchase has been satisfactory. All associates get a list of five to ten customers to call every month. The associates get small incentive rewards for completing their lists, but the calling isn't seen as a chore. It's a way to connect with customers.

Every Lexus employee who comes into contact with customers—which means virtually everyone—is indoctrinated in the Lexus covenant. Before they appear in a Lexus showroom sales associates are enrolled in the Lexus Promise class on their way to formal certification. For openers, Lexus sales associates, unlike those at many luxury-car dealers, don't look at potential customers with a jaundiced eye, seeming skeptical of their wherewithal or insinuating that they should be grateful just to get a test-drive. Instead, Lexus dealers and sales associates welcome potential customers as they would guests to their homes, and they will go to great lengths to solve customer problems—whatever they may be.

Mechanics go to a regional training facility for an intensive course in the car's innards. To increase their commitment to the company and its product line master certified associates are offered special terms to lease a Lexus for their own use.

The entire corporate culture is tuned to respond instantly and unhesitatingly to any customer who has a problem, no matter what it may be. Jill Dittrick recalls a conversation with a second-time Lexus buyer who was thrilled with everything about the car and delighted with the whole transaction. But she did have a favor to ask: Having left her favorite cassette tape in the old car, she wondered if someone could get it back for her.

Jill immediately called the customer satisfaction group, which in turn immediately called the dealer, whose technicians found the tape and sent it to the customer. The point of the story, she says, is that it isn't unusual. Customers make such requests all the time, and "people don't balk at things like that," she says. "They don't say, 'We can't do that, we can't get that thing back.' They just think, 'Okay, let's see if we can find it.'"

Like everything else at Lexus, the Human TouchPoint is also evolving with the brand. After the New Luxury Tour, dealers around the country worked to involve their employees in finding new ways to improve the Lexus standard of service. A dealer in Tucson, Arizona, for instance, set up a "luxury enrichment team"; the team took the lead in renovating the customer lounge and installing new exterior lighting that made the dealership more visible at night.

At Park Place Lexus in Plano, Texas, a similar committee of a dozen employees is called the 50/50 Program; it's responsible both for spotting problems and finding solutions. The committee has come up with ideas large and small, from reducing waiting time for customer service to offering classes in English as a second language for Spanish-speaking employees to help them develop new skills and earn promotions. "You can truly see the pride and loyalty they have for Park Place," says Wendy Simmons, the dealership's human resources manager, and that, she says, "ultimately translates to our customers." Building on its success, early in 2004 the dealership started offering courses in Spanish as a second language, on the theory that the classes would facilitate bonding among its employees and help the English speakers better relate to the Spanish-speaking community. Basically, says president Jordan Case, "We're sending the message that we care about our associates"—and that can only help in the endless process of strengthening the Human TouchPoint for the customers.

TouchPoints Survive the Test

If Lexus is confident and sure-footed it's because all of its Touch-Points have been battle tested. Early in its history the division survived a challenging situation that could have spelled disaster.

In September 1989 just eight thousand of the newly introduced LS 400 cars were on the road. Their buyers had been promised nothing less than perfection. But suddenly flaws appeared. First, an owner in Texas discovered defective housing in his center rear brake light. Then, within a matter of days, the twenty-four-hour roadside-assistance program reported two more problems: a dead battery and a locked-up cruise-control system.

What to do? A recall would easily fix modelwide problems—if that's what they were. But the plastic brake-light housing appeared to have gone soft in the Texas sun, and the battery died because of a loose alternator connection, while the cruise control failed because of a supplier's faulty actuator. If these problems had come after years of a good track record a recall could have been shrugged off. But, as Dave Illingworth remembers, the general question was: "Do we really need to do this? Maybe this was just a one-case thing. Do we dare risk a safety recall on the 'perfect' car under these circumstances?"

It didn't take long to make the decision. "Everybody realized we had to step up and take our licks," says Illingworth. "A lot of people will make fun of us. The competition is going to have a field day with this. But the one thing we will do is take care of the people that bought the car." On December 1 a "special service campaign" was announced. If they manage it right, thought Yuki Togo, "this can make us stronger. It seems like bad luck, but we can turn it into good luck."

But Togo's optimistic outcome didn't seem likely, at least not at first. Such recalls can take a year to complete, yet service manager Dick Chitty wanted this one done in twenty days, before Christmas. Production of the replacement parts had to be ramped up and a training video prepared for the mechanics. Dealers were encouraged to warn owners personally, before the official letters went out, and elaborate plans were made to service the cars of the many customers who lived more than two hundred miles from their dealers.

"Oh my God, here comes trouble," said a Midwestern dealer, and sure enough, the reaction was fierce. "Yes, the Japanese are human too," wrote the *Los Angeles Times*. *Automotive News* noted dryly that rival luxury car makers were "amused," and the *Wall Street Journal* warned that the recall was "certain to hurt" the Lexus image.

But Lexus mobilized all its System and Human TouchPoints to deal with the crisis. Engineers were flown in from Japan. Managers in Torrance were sent off to dealerships to lend a hand. Every technician was assigned overtime work for the duration. Dealers hired extra mechanics, kept their service bays open far into the night, and rounded up new cars to use as loaners for customers inconvenienced by the recall. Many owners had their cars picked up and delivered by dealers, who assigned sales personnel as drivers in the emergency. Some customers found a rose on the dashboard when their cars came back.

All the owners in remote locations got house calls from technicians who were crisscrossing the country. (A mechanic was flown to Alaska to service the state's one Lexus, which luckily was in Anchorage and not in the boondocks.) The technicians did the repairs at a local Toyota dealership if there was one; if not, they rented space at an independent repair shop. Lacking any facility, they fixed the car in the owner's garage or driveway. Their orders were to contact the customer, get the job done the best way they could, get the car washed, and hand it back to the owner with a full tank of gas. If the tank was already full, they were instructed to give the owner a check for a full tank of premium fuel.

The operations manager of the Western area training facility at Irvine, California, spent two crisis weeks on the road. He remembers finding one owner hang gliding in the middle of the Mojave Desert. He did the repairs, but couldn't find a car wash in the area—a Lincoln dealer had one but wouldn't let him use it. So he left a twenty-dollar bill on the dashboard with a note of apology. Chitty later told the operations manager that the owner called to say "he never had a rep who fixed his car, filled it with gas, and left money."

In the end, all the repairs were completed by December 20—and Lexus was, indeed, stronger for the whole incident. What could have been a disaster became a triumph of customer relations, and the month's sales figures actually rose to summer levels. "People could not believe what happened to their neighbors and their friends," says Carl Sewell, a dealer in Texas. "It turned out to be such a positive." *Time* wrote that the recall campaign was a lesson in "Zen and the Art of Automobile Maintenance," and concluded: "Lexus has created virtually instant brand loyalty, a feat unprecedented in the luxury-auto market."

It has been said that perfection is a journey, not a destination. But Lexus is clearly intent on putting the lie to such silly pessimism. The desire to live up to its brand promise and achieve flawless performance at every level of its operation truly inspires this company and its employees. Lexus exemplifies TouchPoint Branding at its very best.

CONCLUSION

YOU ARE NOW PREPARED to assume the mantle of TouchPoint Brander. Whether you are a new company preparing to jump into the competitive fray for the first time or a seasoned veteran in need of an overhaul to maintain your edge, the case studies I have presented and the suggestions I have made in this book should enable you to overpromise and overdeliver. By designing a new and unique brand promise, coupled with a continuing commitment to making the most of your Product, System, and Human TouchPoints, you will gain an advantage over your competitors. And like the market leaders whose stories have informed my methodology, your determination will be rewarded. You, your company, and your brand will join the elite ranks of those who overpromise and overdeliver.

This book provides a blueprint for TouchPoint Branding. All that's left is execution. Which is where you come in. Let me know how it's going. You can reach me at rick.barrera@overpromise.com.

Index